# U2

*the*
# Complete
# Guide *to their*
# Music

**OMNIBUS PRESS**
London/New York
Paris/Sydney/Copenhagen
Berlin/Madrid/Tokyo

**Bill Graham &
Caroline
van Oosten de Boer**

Cover and book designed by Chloë Alexander
Picture research by Sarah Bacon

ISBN: 0.7119.9886.8
Order No: OP 49533

Exclusive Distributors
Book Sales Limited
8/9 Frith Street,
London W1D 3JB, UK.

Music Sales Corporation
257 Park Avenue South,
New York, NY 10010, USA.

Music Sales Pty Limited,
120 Rothschild Avenue, Rosebery,
NSW 2018, Australia.

To the Music Trade only:
Music Sales Limited,
8/9, Frith Street,
London W1D 3JB, UK.

Every effort has been made to trace the copyright holders
of the photographs in this book but one or two were
unreachable. We would be grateful if the photographers
concerned would contact us.

Printed by: Cox & Wyman Ltd, Reading, Berks.

A catalogue record for this book is available from the
British Library.

Visit Omnibus Press at http://www.musicsales.co.uk

# Contents

# INTRODUCTION

**U**<sup></sup>**2 FIRST FOUND FAME AS A LIVE BAND. BONO'S SHOWMANSHIP AND ACUTE** sense of his audience, Edge's repetitive yet resonant guitar and the dedicated professionalism of the band and their entourage meant U2 always had a head-start over their contemporaries in any race for stadium status.

But such origins haven't always helped their reputation as recording artists. Recent critical arguments have more often raged over symbolic issues like their Irishness, their religious and political beliefs or the band's canny reluctance to steer their career according to any of the short-lived manifestos of the Eighties. U2 seem to encourage only extreme ends of appraisal; heroes or charlatans, coloured in black and white and rarely viewed in any shades of grey. Far more than most superstar acts, they've rarely received critical coverage that's neither worshipful nor damning. Consequently, their music has often been drowned in the critical din.

But check through all their albums and you find a band of versatility with an extraordinary capacity for evolution. The eager baby band, the irresistibly ambitious performance act of their first incarnation, is now a memory. From *The Unforgettable Fire* through to *Zooropa*, no act of their generation has released such a broad range of music. Is it really the self-same quartet who are responsible for tracks as diverse as 'A Sort Of Homecoming' and 'Numb', 'Love Is Blindness' and 'Angel Of Harlem'?

And U2 are a band. Obviously Edge and Bono grab the bulk of the attention as the band's creative sorcerers but Adam Clayton and Larry Mullen should never be dismissed as their apprentices. Indeed, they must surely now be rated among rock's classic rhythm sections, a pair who've given the confidence and context – personally stable but creatively fluid – for Bono and Edge to follow their dreams. Publicists often exaggerate the solidarity and mutual interdependence of young bands but in the case of U2, the evidence of 15 years together proves the point.

Initially Bono and Edge were more effective allies on stage than on record. For all his audacity as a performer, Bono wasn't always comfortable singing in the studio. He could get impatient, dealing with the tedious routine of take after take in a sterile, windowless room. Edge, on the other hand, was captivated by the sonic potential of the modern studio, and from the outset he approached it as an additional instrument in the band's arsenal.

Gradually U2 found a superior energy. Their music became a world tour of discovery, continent-hopping back and forth across the Atlantic from America to Europe. Both expanded their skills and Edge graduated from being just another promising young guitar whiz to the orchestrator of the band's sound, a master of both rhythm and melody, equipped with a bewildering armoury of skills.

In a previous book about U2's earliest days in Ireland, I stole a line from John Berger, writing about the great Irish painter and the poet's brother, Jack Yeats. In this 1958 essay, he wrote: 'Ireland has not yet reached that critical point where she can only defend her way of life: she is still striving, staggering, suffering and dreaming her way towards one... it is impossible to appreciate Yeats without understanding something of this.'

So with U2 and their dizzy sense of mission, even if it's sometimes involved rediscovering old ideas their seniors have cast aside. But recycling is acceptable if it also renews and reinvents. Certainly John Berger's lines about Jack Yeats still go some way to explain U2's intense and continuing sense of artistic vocation. They've been fuelled by faith but they've never forgotten the other two cardinal virtues of hope and charity.

And unlike so many in rock's second generation, they've had the wit and resolution never to be false and fearful suburban Bohemians, flinching from the future. I hope this book serves to show how U2 were always running and never standing still.

*Bill Graham, January 1996.*

---

Sadly Bill Graham, the original author of this book died in 1996.
Analysis of U2's work from November 1995, including compilation records, onwards has been written by Caroline van Oosten de Boer

---

# Boy

Island ILPS 9646; released November 1980

**B**OY OPENED U2'S CAREER WITH A WHOOP AND A WHIRL. PART OF THE PUNK manifesto was that rock music be reopened to the young, but too many art-school nostrums often gave its albums a degree of self-consciousness and knowingness that was truer to its listeners' aspirations of hipness than their experiences of adolescent insecurity.

But the secret of *Boy* was that U2 refused to grow up too fast. The *Boy* was still on the cusp of manhood. He didn't fake a false self-confidence that he didn't really feel deep inside. He might be gushingly romantic but he was also hopelessly confused about girls and all his new responsibilities as he quit the family unit.

This theme makes *Boy* unique since rock'n'roll has always pretended to be more grown up than it really was. Its rites of passage emphasise the 'after' not the 'before' and most rockers might have felt that Bono's behaviour in mourning his mother was cissy. Rock generally finished adolescence with a mask but *Boy* was original in that it stripped it off.

Lypton Village, the teenage clan of school and street friends from Bono's neighbourhood of North Dublin, was responsible for this. Among its most defining traits was an intolerance of laddishness, the premature fake masculinity of 'hard men' whether they played sports or heavy metal. Bono would emphasise his emotional vulnerability and his earliest stage character would be 'The Fool', a hyperactively confused creation, intentionally portrayed without an ounce of cool. But then *Boy* was almost therapy for Bono. The death of his mother when he was 14 was still the dominant experience of his life.

*Boy* also discarded many of the hip distractions of the era. When it was released British post-punk music was a bazaar of competing styles. The new mods, Oi, the synth innovators of industrial music and ska were all vying for attention against the surviving punk originators. The achievement of *Boy* is that U2 refused to dress up as the dummies of post-punk ventriloquism. They determined to start from scratch on the only Dublin ground they knew. From U2's viewpoint, that might be the real meaning of the Blank Generation.

Of course, their music wasn't totally devoid of influences or precedents. Bono's singing may be breathless but he still can't rid the ghost of David Bowie from his throat. Both then and since, Edge has always acknowledged the primary influence of Television's Tom Verlaine on his playing.

Besides, a stylist like Edge was probably inevitable in the aftermath of punk. The single might still be more dominant than the album, but the three-piece unit had to develop from the fundamental and speeded-up hard rock riffing of primitive punk bands like Penetration (another accepted influence), The Skids, Siouxsie And The Banshees, The Cure and their immediate contemporaries Echo & The Bunnymen. They were definitely merging lead and rhythm guitar in a new, more colourful style that was to be falsely if conveniently dubbed neo-psychedelic. Edge caught that wave but then surfed away on his own.

But it's obvious that U2 weren't neo-anything. At their songwriting rehearsals they were always determined to avoid any borrowed licks. But this wasn't just stylistic stubbornness. For whatever Irish reason, U2 had a different mood and agenda. Unlike The Clash, U2 weren't the last gang in town. They were romantics who knew nothing of the self-conscious decadence that infected much of the British punk and post-punk scenes. In the comparatively unhip confines of Dublin in the late Seventies, fashion was neither a friend nor a temptation.

There was a further reason for the album's freshness. In time-warped Ireland, rock was still a dream. The first generational battles for rock culture that had long been won in America and Britain were still being fought in Ireland. Punks elsewhere could be considered the second or third generation of rock but, in Ireland, U2 could still count themselves among the pathfinders of the first.

Perhaps that's why their early production association with Martin Hannett didn't work. That single session did produce their original Island single, 'One O'Clock Tick Tock', but there was little common social ground between the Mancunian and a U2 that was now entering its Christian phase (even if it's far from marked from Bono's lyrics which had been written before that fascination really caught hold).

Instead, Steve Lillywhite took charge, an ideal elder brother with his own brand of fresh enthusiasm to initiate the quartet into the mysteries of the recording process. And unlike earlier Irish bands, U2 had another advantage in the foundation of Dublin's Windmill Studio. As a result, they would be Windmill's special, cherished clients who didn't have to make their début in an alien and potentially distracting environment.

Essentially Lillywhite was a facilitator. The songs on *Boy* had already been proven live and so the arrangements needed little re-routing. Edge's playing is usually single rather than multitracked, and most of the work was spent on tidying up the timing of Larry Mullen and Adam Clayton.

Of course, *Boy* has its blemishes. U2 were still apprentice songwriters and they are prone to repetition on the faster material, a problem not fully eradicated until *The Unforgettable Fire*. But 'The Ocean', 'Shadows And Tall Trees' and, especially, the sequence of 'An Cat Dubh' and 'Into The Heart' more than hint at their later lyricism.

## I WILL FOLLOW

EDGE SURGES in for the first time, Lillywhite adds a glockenspiel flavour and the album-buying public get their first experience of U2's racing exuberance. From the start, the quartet are true to the theme of the album. Bono's back in childhood memories when 'his mother takes him by the hand'. Could we just be hearing the first phase of a common theme, painful separation from the Loved One, followed by a search when he never knows whether he prefers to be 'with or without you'.

## TWILIGHT

A SONG OF some suburban mystery of initiation, Bono's lyrics were even then symbolic rather than specific, without the hip details that might date them. All we know is that he's trying to avoid his father's protection, caught up 'in the shadow (where) boy meets man'. His vocals are uncertain, rushed and almost gulping, whereas Edge is more assured. Towards the end, we get a very early example of his ability to orchestrate U2 through a set of three different, driving, melodic passages.

## AN CAT DUBH/ INTO THE HEART

SEPARATED on the track listing but these two songs are segued together and were always played that way live. The first track to reveal that U2 might have a magic beyond teenage enthusiasm, I first heard it echoing around Hammersmith Clarendon in the early summer of 1980. Edge's original guitar construction was hardly changed on record and Lillywhite's production concentrated on emphasising Larry's drum parts.

But this is exemplary Edge. Instead of taking 'An Cat Dubh' to any clichéd climax, he, Larry and Adam turn the dynamics down before the new melody shyly emerges to introduce 'Into The Heart'. His elders had neither the grasp of dynamics nor the ability to produce a melody of such emotive richness and strength. Meanwhile, still mourning lost innocence and the destruction of the secret garden of youth, Bono chants 'into the heart of a child'. Non-Irish speakers should know that 'An Cat Dubh' means 'the black cat'.

## OUT OF CONTROL

DRUMS kick in but again the dynamics are deceptive. Bono's character, The Fool, should hurtle through this song but instead, just before the three minute mark, he and the music are reined back. Edge doodles on the verges and Bono's vocal dissolves in dreamy echoes on the outskirts of the track. A slight but significant revision of the stage original to ensure the album wouldn't get too predictable.

## STORIES FOR BOYS

A VERY EARLY song with a sort of toy town suburban punk feel. Like 'Out Of Control', the lyrics undermine laddish male stereotypes. U2 will write their own 'stories for boys'.

## THE OCEAN

A CAMEO, but also the earliest example of how U2 could alchemise apparent fragments and drone into the most special moments. Even then, U2 had the taste to underplay, though those gifts were often ignored until *The Unforgettable Fire*. The Boy wishes to merge with the universe but can't as he sits by the sea, 'a picture in grey, Dorian Gray.'

Obviously, even then Bono was reading the Oscar Wilde books that belonged to his soulmate, Gavin Friday of The Virgin Prunes.

## A DAY WITHOUT ME

R ELEASED as a single after their mutual try-out session with Steve Lillywhite, this was U2's first attempt to be Stars on 45 but they still hadn't found the knack of blending their own peculiar sound with what radio required. Oddly, 'A Day Without Me' is deceptively jaunty since suicide is among its themes. The first sign of an early fault: U2's themes and rhymes don't always merge.

## ANOTHER TIME, ANOTHER PLACE

N OTHING to do with Bryan Ferry unless it was a product of Lypton Village's collective unconscious. 'With a tear on my tongue', Bono's again refusing to play the fake male and still languishing on the borderlands of adulthood where 'another child has lost the race'.

## THE ELECTRIC CO.

A LATER live favourite, the title's pun doesn't only refer to a rock band but also ECT – 'the toy could feel a hole in your head' – an especially favoured practice of Irish shrinks for existentially dazed teenagers in that era. The band slam in but the definitive version must be on *Under A Blood Red Sky*.

## SHADOWS AND TALL TREES

T HE TRACK most revised from its early live version. This ballad was in the earliest U2 set I witnessed, but Edge's original florid solo is set aside for a more democratic arrangement that ranks Adam and Larry higher in the mix. The reason: band and producer may have felt the original got dangerously close to soft-metal. As for Bono, he gets to tell the story on yet another lyric that accepts that adolescent angst and autonomy are effectively inseparable.

# October

Island ILPS 9680; released October 1981

**I**N THE PECKING ORDER OF **U2** ALBUMS, *OCTOBER* HAS LONG BEEN THE RUNT OF
the litter, lacking even the landmark prestige of the début. Even in commercial terms, it was a partial failure since it hardly added to the audience U2 had gained by their touring and through Boy.

The reasons for its demotion aren't that hard to detect. *October* is patchy and sounds hurried. U2 are eager and willing but they were still learning their craft. Good ideas aren't always followed through.

It both lost and gained through U2's arduous touring schedule. As with any début, *Boy* was the selective product of the band's best early material but with the follow-up U2 had to show they could cope with the pressures of starting from scratch. Nor had their preparations been helped by an incident on the West Coat when Bono lost a briefcase with all his notes for lyrics. On the other hand, touring was an education that exposed U2 to new experiences. Furthermore, if U2 had lost some of the tousle-headed innocence of *Boy*, touring was starting to lend a new aggression to their playing.

But the real change was that U2, or at least the trio of Bono, Edge and Larry, had come out as Christians. It wasn't officially announced in so many words, the band still preferred to steer away from the topic in their interviews, and October is the lone U2 album without even one lyric in the packaging. Nevertheless, songs like 'Gloria' and 'October' were highly explicit about the beliefs that were guiding the band, while 'Rejoice', 'With A Shout' and 'Scarlet' are also saturated with Christian sentiment and imagery.

Suspicions about their Christianity would create insuperable obstacles to their acceptance in many quarters but, paradoxically, their beliefs would eventually have a positive creative impact. Christianity would shelter them against early injurious influences, sustain their idealism and working discipline, and protect U2 against the worst vice that can threaten a young band: the corruption of premature cynicism. Outsiders looking in were also prone to mistake their Christianity for traditional Irish Catholicism and miss a most crucial distinction. They would pass through a zealous phase but, essentially, U2's faith was inclusive not exclusive, flexible and charitable not dogmatic. A band who played a benefit for family planning groups who opposed Ireland's rigid laws against contraception could hardly be indicted for illiberal Puritanism.

Born-again Christianity would also offer U2 creative advantages they couldn't yet foresee. British rock writing, as exemplified by the massive influence of *New Musical Express* and *Melody Maker* in the late Seventies and early Eighties, concentrated on the secular and was often uncomfortable or embarrassed with the spiritual which was associated with Cliff Richard and Pat Boone, the milksop doctrines of establishment Anglicanism, hellfire Dixie preachers or the exotic, erotic disciplines of Catholicism. Many, though not all, writers approaching Bob Marley's Rastafarianism would mention ganja and anti-imperialist politics but refrain from inquiring about its spiritual essence.

But John Lennon, Bob Dylan and Van Morrison had already shown rock had its spiritual side. Choosing Christianity immunised U2 against the worst hippie excesses of ersatz Eastern religion and New Age fakery and kept them within the broad terms of Western culture. Their religious beliefs would offer U2 a unique perspective into the spiritual conflicts of American rock, soul, gospel and even the jazz of John Coltrane. The trio of Bono, Edge and Larry hardly decided to be baptised in the Blood of the Lamb for these insights but they would eventually gain from them all the same.

But they hadn't made those discoveries before recording *October*. Instead U2 were striving to progress beyond the original blueprint of *Boy*. New song forms are explored, Edge started playing piano and that led to the title track, the album's one enduring triumph. Steve Lillywhite's production sought new variations in the band's dynamics by giving extra exposure to Adam and Larry, but there are also moments when the band's hurtling, headlong style seems less sparkling and an increasingly compulsive bad habit. The adrenalin boost of touring isn't always dampened down. But listen closely and you can hear the sprouting of the seeds that would be harvested on later albums.

---

## GLORIA

THEY COULD hardly have been less overt about their Christian beliefs as Bono chanted the opening cut's Latin chorus, 'Gloria, exultat me'. The music is equally exuberant and buoyant on what would be their second single from the album and its live stand-out, a song that would endure as a concert showcase right up to the 1994 Zooropa tour. Adam gets his first chance to thump out a bass solo as glass shatters in the background.

## I FALL DOWN

THE ALBUM'S first attempt to escape their prototype sound, Edge moves to piano and acoustic guitar as U2 try their hand at pretty pop akin to Julian Cope's Teardrop Explodes. Many early songs were quickly discarded from their live set as U2 developed, but 'I Fall Down' was a lost miniature that didn't deserve that fate. A sweet aperitif if not yet the main course.

## I THREW A BRICK THROUGH A WINDOW

WITH DUB-STYLE bass and a galumping drum break at the end, the first evidence of U2 and Steve Lillywhite's efforts to rejig the band's dynamics. Bono's hesitating, looking at his face in the mirror, disliking it and ready to externalise his anger in a lyric of typical adolescent confusion. The song can seem equally hesitant in its changes with Edge's clarion guitar part its most finished moment.

## REJOICE

THE CHRISTIAN theme returns. Bono testifies 'I can't change the world but I can change the world in me' on a track that's perhaps too hurtling and breathless. Note, though, how touring America had given Edge a dirtier sound.

## FIRE

ALL OTHER tracks had been recorded at Windmill but 'Fire', released as a single three months before the album, was cut at an earlier session in Nassau during a break from the band's American expedition. Starting with some mock-choral vocal harmonies, 'Fire' was another effort to adapt the band's sound and excitement for a more conservative radio environment but somehow it rarely delivers on the promise of its first verse. Too often, U2 were still a one-gear band.

## TOMORROW

THE TRACK on the album that most encapsulates what was bad and good about U2 at this point. For the first time in their career, U2 fly the flag for Irish music as Vinnie Kilduff's uilleann pipes cast off for the skies. Scenic, cinematic *and* Bono's singing is appropriately soulful but then at mid-point the mood is killed and the spell is lost as the rest of the band crudely clatter in and the tempo changes to a sprint.

Bono justified this change through the lyric which moved from haunted memories of his mother's funeral to the theme of fear and violence in Northern Ireland. But, typically for a young band, U2 were still prone to mistakenly and automatically equate passion with rock'n'roll velocity.

## OCTOBER

HERE U2 don't commit the disfiguring mistake of 'Tomorrow' and so 'October' was the second great survivor from this album, later re-appearing, embellished by Wally Badarou's keyboards, on the soundtrack for an Island film, *They Call It An Accident*.

Edge's piano melody is outstandingly precocious, then Bono drifts in with the lyrics – 'October, and kingdoms rise and kingdoms fall, but you go on and on' – an unabashed and naked display of faith in the Spirit that moves all things.

For the times, it's a remarkable display of artistic courage, the clearest instance so far of U2's determination to stare down the fashion police. Yet its mysterious artistry takes it far beyond any point of principle. How could such a young band achieve such simplicity and enduring depth of emotion?

## WITH A SHOUT

U2 UP THE tempo again but this time experiment with dance rhythms, drawing in a brief blast from the horns of a Dublin band of the period, Some Kind Of Wonderful. Again Christian themes are to the fore with Bono fixated on Jerusalem and the crucifixion 'on the side of a hill (where) blood was spilled'.

## STRANGER IN A STRANGE LAND

TAKING ITS title from the Robert Heinlein novel which inspired *The Man Who Fell To Earth*, David Bowie's first starring role as a movie actor, this could have been inspired by their American experiences except that the second verse about an encounter with a soldier seems closer to home and Northern Ireland. Again the music's in stop-start mode, caught between hesitation and acceleration but Bono's singing, especially on the chorus, is persuasively confidential while the lyric was his most finished narrative so far. Better than any track on

'October', this captures their confusion and their growing pains.

## SCARLET

THE EARLIEST example of the U2 droned chant, 'Scarlet' can be heard as a rehearsal for '40'. Again Edge's piano conducts the mood. This and similar tracks on the album had been influenced by albums of Gregorian chants given to them by their manager, Paul McGuinness.

## IS THAT ALL?

AND REALLY, *October* should have finished with 'Scarlet'. This is filler. Edge's riff is inventive but there's no sense of where to direct it and Steve Lillywhite's elevation of Larry's drums seem more product cosmetics than any useful manipulation of the dynamics.

# War

Island ILPS 9733; released March 1983

**W**AR WAS U2'S FIRST COMMERCIAL SUCCESS, A CHART-TOPPING ALBUM IN the UK and elsewhere in Europe that also included their first hit single, 'New Year's Day'. It was the album that justified their tireless touring. Through their intense live shows, U2 had now won their own fiercely loyal audience, ready to flock to the shops in the first days of its release.

But their first major seller still had artistic flaws, especially on its later tracks. *War* often lacks composure and the band aren't always certain of their direction. It has bags of precocious ideas but sometimes they misfire as the old U2 and any number of potential new U2's jostle for space.

The pressure shows. After their first two introductory albums, *War* had to be the breakthrough for a band deep in debt to their record company. Nor did it help that the three Christian members of U2 were deeply torn between the conflicting demands of their careers and their religious beliefs. At one critical point, Edge was almost tempted to quit. *War* can be incoherent but it rarely lacks intensity.

Then there was the context of the times. The album was written and recorded in the last third of 1982 when post-punk rock was under threat. The New Romantics and synth-pop had begun their rise and the unadorned sincerity of U2's music was at odds with the new fops of fashion-pop. *War* would feature Edge's most rugged and spikiest guitar yet, an intentional slap in the face to the cooler values of the new keyboard-saturated pop. Some would also deem it a diplomatic gesture to their new American fans.

But there were other musical advances. Adam and Larry's playing was also more muscular and assertive but sometimes they get in the way. Adam especially had saturated himself in reggae and funk records from the Island larder but sometimes it can sound as if the rhythm pair are trying too hard to prove themselves and deflecting The Edge.

Clayton's relationship with his three partners had also been at its most frayed during the tour that preceded *War*. Excluded from their prayer meetings, he felt isolated and may have unconsciously over-compensated in his playing. Eleven years later, Bono would also admit 'the uptightness of that album is something I feel – tight, taut, choked, words choked, not singing them well.'

But you can also hear early sketches of *The Unforgettable Fire* sound in the guitar, keyboard and vocal harmony layerings that often get drowned out in the din. Producing U2 for the third time, Steve Lillywhite had a hard job as referee.

Indeed Lillywhite hadn't intended to officiate. He had a firm rule that he never produced more than two albums with any one artist. But sessions with Blondie's keyboard player, Jimmy Destri, and Sandy Pearlman (Blue Oyster Cult, Clash) didn't pan out, while Roxy Music's Rhett Davies was rejected for being too much of a neutral engineer. With recording deadlines fast approaching, Lillywhite changed his usual policy to help his friends out of a hole.

The result was an album that sometimes oversells itself, while U2's lyrical side was temporarily abandoned. While contemporary Liverpool rivals, Echo & The Bunnymen were exploring *Heaven Up Here*, U2 set aside the sound of 'An Cat Dubh'/'Into The Light' and 'October'.

But *War* is far from an artistic desert. Besides 'New Year's Day', it also provided two enduring show stoppers in 'Sunday Bloody Sunday' and '40'. Bono's lyrics were maturing as adolescent themes became replaced by meatier adult matters. *War* wasn't as political as both its critics and champions claimed but U2 were now definitely testing their beliefs in the public arena.

Paradoxically, the album that made U2 commercial thoroughbreds was also something of an artistic mongrel. Still, as so often with U2, the seeds of future successes can be heard in earlier failures.

---

## SUNDAY BLOODY SUNDAY

MODERN Irish history has two Bloody Sundays. The first was the calculated killing of British undercover agents by Michael Collins' original I.R.A. in 1920. This led to an unprovoked revenge attack on a defenceless football crowd by the Crown forces at Dublin's Croke Park (where U2 would play) later that afternoon. Then in 1972, the British parachute regiment became the I.R.A.'s most effective recruiting agents by shooting 13 unarmed marchers at a Civil Rights parade in Derry.

But U2's song doesn't comment directly on those case-histories of atrocity. Often flagged as their début as political philosophers, this peace-anthem struggles to express the pain and futility of the Northern Ireland Troubles but takes no sides other than to stress the pointlessness of sectarian violence and hatred, the never-ending tragedy focused by the question 'How long must we sing this song?' which would be echoed later in the album's closing song, '40'.

U2 had a peculiar perspective since they had neither a Northern nor, with the exception of Larry and Bono's fathers, a Catholic background. The notion of religion as a dividing force they found both incomprehensible and inexcusable. But this Christian witness and call for reconciliation, with its passionate neutrality above the warring factions, often offended those sympathetic to the Republican cause.

In some ways, it was intended

to. Touring America in the previous year, U2 had been pressurised to support the I.R.A. hunger strikers in Long Kesh although they were unwilling. Writing the basic song in New York, Bono had always intended it wouldn't be 'a rebel song'.

This was controversial given the passions inflamed by the hunger strike. Folk acts like Moving Hearts and Christy Moore did support the prisoners but Irish rock took its lead from the Belfast punk scene led by Stiff Little Fingers and the local Good Vibrations Attitudes there were far more ambivalent and few wished to threaten the non-sectarian space that punk had created. U2 held the same sympathies. Moreover, if outside of Ireland U2's religious beliefs might bewilder rock insiders, 'Sunday Bloody Sunday' proved they could be a definite artistic advantage in their homeland.

But this peace song has mostly martial rhythms as Larry Mullin takes from his own (peaceful) Dublin pipe-band apprenticeship and U2 become their own Salvation Army band. Guest fiddler, Steve Wickham, soon to join In Tua Nua and later, The Waterboys, adds some dramatic streaks to the sound and then joins Edge in a nervily jolting rhythm part above the Mullin strut.

'Sunday Bloody Sunday' doesn't hesitantly implore; instead it insists on peace with all the certainty of youth. Bob Marley, an obvious background influence on Bono, wasn't the only Island artist pleading for One Love.

## SECONDS

THE FIRST U2 song on which Edge sings lead. And yet he sounds uncannily like Bono on this anti-nuclear lament that also includes a brief sample from the documentary movie, *Soldier Girls*. Not dissimilarly structured to 'Sunday Bloody Sunday', Adam funks it up against essentially acoustic playing from Edge but its chief interest is a blurred harmony part. It's hardly as lavish as *The Unforgettable Fire* but it is the first clue to their later development. Meanwhile the lyrical pun about 'where they dance the atomic bomb' refers to Washington D.C. labelmates, Troublefunk.

## NEW YEAR'S DAY

THEIR FIRST hit single alluded to the Polish Solidarity movement but it was partially coincidence. The song was already written and being recorded when U2 learned the news that the Polish régime would end martial law on New Year's Day 1983. The lyrics fit, though the song could be about love in any cold and emotionally and politically oppressive climate. Still, I've always wondered if all the snow imagery in the video and the second line – 'a world in white gets underway' – might have been affected by the weather of January 1982 when Ireland and especially Dublin suffered its worst snowfalls in living memory.

The song's main musical attraction was Edge's racing keyboard melody – again an anticipation of *The Unforgettable Fire* – that leads off a surging tour de force of a guitar solo. Later a regular show stealer in concert, it is his finest moment so far. Nobody made fretboard logic so exciting.

## LIKE A SONG

A CONTRADICTORY cut since this isn't so much a song as U2 by rote. Certainly it's not like a song at its climax. The Edge digs out the rhythm, Larry Mullin's drums are thunderously over-dubbed, but it still sounds as if all concerned are striving for effect to make up for the lack of better inspirations.

## DROWNING MAN

B ONO'S Christianity gave him one unconsidered psychological advantage in the stardom stakes: it saved him the usual ego and identity problems since he thought his inspiration came from, and was meant to serve, a higher power. It also made his lyrics unusually open-ended. 'Drowning Man' explores the themes of 'egolessness' and self-surrender to a higher love. But were his love songs to Christ, his wife Ali, or a metaphor of U2's own relationship with their audience?

It's also the song Bono still favours from the album; perhaps because it also admits a sense of confusion, half-aware that their rigid style of belief was becoming emotional armour.

Again this is a schizophrenic track. Edge moves from acoustic

guitar to find new echoes in his effects palette, but the mood gets overpowered by Adam Clayton's bottom-heavy bass. U2 can seem to be trying too hard but then Steve Wickham's violin, another hint to the orchestrations of *The Unforgettable Fire*, wafts in to soothe their troubles.

## THE REFUGEE

A NOTHER anomaly. Steve Lillywhite did confer the final mix but this is a demo track produced by Bill Whelan, an Irishman who'd played with folk-fusioneers, Moving Hearts. Even before Brian Eno's arrival, this is U2 straying into Talking Heads territory, the music canoeing upriver against the current of Larry's mock-tribal drums.

A real oddity as U2 try on clothes that don't yet really suit them, 'Refugee' attempts to parallel the Irish emigrant experience in America with those of Afro-Americans. From one angle, preposterous; from another, the sort of brave juvenilia all bands need to risk to progress.

## TWO HEARTS BEAT AS ONE

T HE SECOND single from the album, U2 take aim at rock-dance but it doesn't fully work. Still the cut bustles along merrily, Edge plays some striking rhythm guitar as Bono harks back to the school disco – 'I can't stop the dance/this must be my last chance'. Points for energy, not form.

## RED LIGHT

PLAYING A Dublin date at the time, Kid Creole's Coconuts and their trumpeter, Kenny Fradley, were enlisted as aides. But their icing can't save a bad cake. The riffs are pasted together and the joins are transparent. The weakest track.

## SURRENDER

THE ALBUM'S companion to 'Drowning Man' as Bono again searches for selflessness and tries to crack the ego. Chunky guitars dissolve into the swooning atmospherics of the chorus. Again U2 are reaching for a new sound but just fail to grasp it; again they haven't quite worked out the role of Clayton and Mullen.

## 40

ADAM CLAYTON was absent from the studio when they found the best version of this, so Edge plays both guitar and bass. After an album when the stone was often unyielding for these sculptors, *War* ends in hard-won peace as U2 find simplicity and soul. Bono takes his text from Psalm 40, the record closes on the original lament, 'How long must we sing this song' but the pained inquiry of 'Sunday Bloody Sunday' is resolved into a prayer that would end all their later concerts through the Eighties.

# Under A Blood Red Sky

### Island IMA 3; released November 1983

BY THE MIDDLE OF THEIR 1983 AMERICAN TOUR, U2 WERE ON THE FRINGES OF arena status. Sooner rather than later, they had to release a live album and this 8-track cut-price mini-album was offered in good time for that year's Christmas market. Strangely, though it's linked with the video of the same title, only two of its performances, 'Gloria' and 'Party Girl', come from that legendary June 5 performance at Red Rocks in Arizona.

Instead the band took one track, '11 O'Clock Tick Tock' from a May 6 show at Boston's Orpheum Theater and the remaining five from an August 20 festival date at the Lorelei Amphitheater in St. Goarhausen, Germany, believing they were more developed performances.

Before this, the band had slipped a live track onto the flipsides of three singles. Also, an earlier recording of a March 6, 1981, Paradise Theater Boston show quickly became a collector's item after it had been circulated to American radio stations for promotional purposes. U2 were also already attracting the flattering attentions of the bootleggers so officially this was the first time that fans could legally enjoy an extended live U2 experience. It was also their first project with Jimmy Iovine who would later produce *Rattle And Hum*. More echo, background singing and crowd noise would be his only garnish to the basic tapes.

What buyers heard was that, even in their early days, U2 were one of the few bands around who could genuinely develop studio performances on stage. It also confirmed Edge's resourcefulness and his ability to sustain the complex drama of U2's music without the aid of studio overdubs.

In retrospect, it is perhaps a touch too polished. By the end of 1983, U2 had played 439 documented live shows and they'd now become absolutely confident of their ability to capture and inspire an audience. Quite naturally and necessarily, they'd lost some of their original endearing teenage innocence and breathlessness. Much of the excitement in watching the early U2 live came from seeing Bono gambling, making mistakes and then somehow saving the situation with split-second intuitive recoveries. Now becoming tight, they hadn't quite yet learned how to get loose again although 'Party Girl' is a commendable attempt to busk it on the high-wire.

*Under A Blood Red Sky* presents U2 as fast-maturing performers, the Kennedy machine of Eighties rock rather than the holy fools and gamblers who first left Ireland to search for America. But then how could Bono's attention-grabbing but high-risk antics be conveyed on record?

---

## GLORIA

FROM RED ROCKS, its choice as the first track shows U2 still weren't backing down on their Christian commitment. The whole performance pivots on Bono's prayer, 'Oh, Lord/If I had anything/Anything at all/I'd give it to you' with the sudden surge of audience frenzy as he exhorts them, 'Up, up, up, I give it to you'. Did the audience appreciate the significance of Bono's plea? Or had the passion of U2's performance sent them past bothering? Meanwhile Adam's funk-bass solo is no longer quite so naked as the studio original.

## 11 O'CLOCK TICK TOCK

A CHANCE to give a home to their orphan track, their début Island single, U2's sole recording with Martin Hannett. A song against post-punk tribalism, inspired by a 1979 concert at Camden's Electric Ballroom when they opened for Orchestral Manoeuvres In The Dark and Talking Heads, it shows how even in their earliest days, Edge and Adam Clayton could integrate a riff so guitar and bass locked together to double its impact. The song also has Virgin Prunes links, its title coming from a note pinned to the door of Bono's home by Gavin Friday after the former had forgotten a meeting.

## I WILL FOLLOW

A SYMBOLIC choice as the first track on their first album. 'A boy tries hard to be a man', Bono had sung then but in the three years since its release, U2 had become adults and this choice can almost be seen as the closing of the first chapter. In fundamentals, it doesn't really stray from the original. The real difference is how Edge could now fill the gaps left open in the studio version.

## PARTY GIRL

U2 LIGHT-HEARTED shock! The band's early intensity often led them to hide the warmer, wittier side of their personalities that their intimates knew. This song whose party girl was Aislinn, Edge's first wife, had originally been released as the B-side to 'A Celebration' in October 1982, titled 'Trash, Trampoline And The Party Girl'. Often used for their set-ending champagne ritual, it's an intentionally informal romp. Hear Edge try a proper guitar solo without his effects and fail!

## SUNDAY BLOODY SUNDAY

A JUSTIFICATION of their choice of the German tracks since it shows how U2 songs could develop live even from the album immediately before. As the flagship song – literally so since Bono paraded around with a white flag – of the *War* tour, U2 had learned what it meant both to themselves and to

their audiences, especially since its peace message had riled Irish-American Republicans.

So the live version sounds both more instrumentally composed and emotionally focused than the original. 'Wipe your tears away' had become Bono's key line and if the original also had a rather busy preceding passage, that bridge was now far more smoothly crossed. Compassion not anger is the bottom line.

## THE ELECTRIC CO.

CERTAINLY the most fiercely played of the earlier songs, this is the track that shows how U2's instrumental trio had bonded. Few bands approached these heights of dynamism till their late Twenties. Then the pace relents and Bono, according to habit, throws in a quote from another song, Stephen Sondheim's 'Send In The Clowns', quipping 'why must I hide from myself when I need a crowd'.

The cap and quote fitted since his earliest stage persona had been 'The Fool', the title of an early unrecorded song. But Sondheim didn't approve; his lawyers sought and won $50,000 in royalties since U2, in a rare oversight, hadn't asked for his consent.

## NEW YEAR'S DAY

PART OF THE real fun is working out how Edge manages to perform both his keyboard and guitar duties. Again the song has an extra vitality after it's been toured especially since both Adam and Larry sound far sharper and closer to the centre of the song.

**40**

IT WAS ON this tour that U2 first developed their trademark closing ceremony with '40' whereby Edge and Adam swapped instruments and the other three members in turn left the stage to leave Larry alone with the audience chanting the refrain. A psalm and a backbeat, this was a reminder that even if by avoiding interviews Mullen had the lowest profile in U2, it was still the drummer who had founded the band.

# The Unforgettable Fire

### Island U25; released October 1984

**T**HERE'S MORE THAN ONE CANDIDATE FOR U2'S BEST ALBUM. HOWEVER, THERE'S little doubt that *The Unforgettable Fire* was their most pivotal album, the coming of age that saved their lives as a creative unit.

Repeating *War* would have been a path to disaster. U2 would have become another formula band with a limited life expectancy. Sooner or later, the inevitable outbreak of 'musical differences' would have divided and destroyed them. And U2 knew this. Immediately after one of the final dates of the *War* tour at Dublin's Phoenix Park, Bono was talking in metaphors about the band breaking up, to re-form again with the same members but a different direction.

But if a break with Steve Lillywhite, with whom they remained fast friends, was inevitable, their choice of replacement, Brian Eno, wasn't. Even their Island boss, the artistically shrewd and open-minded Chris Blackwell was initially uneasy. So was Eno when first approached. He wasn't their original choice. They thought of continuing with Jimmy Iovine but found the first sketches of their new material too European for an American producer. Then they flirted with the idea of approaching Conny Plank before sounding out Eno.

What resolved his early doubts were Bono's powers of persuasion and what he later described as his growing perception of U2's 'lyrical soul in abundance', those very traits that had been smothered on *War*. He noticed that 'they were constantly struggling against it as if they were frightened of being overpowered by some softness'.

As for U2, they also recognised that *War* had been their most rockist and Americanised album. Eno's task was to help them mature a new, more experimental and European musical vocabulary. Edge's long appreciation of Eno's music also prompted U2's decision.

If the U2/Brian Eno relationship is now long established, it seemed a very odd alliance in 1984. But Eno was a far more eclectic character than his Numanoid acolytes of that time realised. He had been a leading inspiration of the industrial synth sound but now he distrusted its increasing artistic aridity, 'the frowning brow over the microphone in harsh white light or dark shadow' syndrome. Moving to New York in the late Seventies, he'd regularly visited Brooklyn's First Baptist Tabernacle of Christ to hear its gospel choir. Now he would remind interviewers that he also was a fan of Hank Williams and even the legendary Irish piper, Seamus Ennis. A lapsed Catholic, Brian Eno too had his sense of soul.

In a 1984 interview with their American radio confidant, Carter Alan, Adam Clayton best expressed the new approach Eno brought. 'With Steve, we were a lot more strict about a song and what it should be; if it did veer off to the left or the right, we would pull back as opposed to chasing it. Brian and Danny were definitely interested in watching where a song went and then chasing it.'

But what nobody had anticipated was that U2 had got two producers for the price of one. Eno's associate, Daniel Lanois, had already won production awards in his native Canada for his work with acts such as Martha & The Muffins. He would be most influential in rerouting the rhythm section, especially in loosening up Larry Mullen's drum patterns.

Probably Edge and Eno would have found an affinity but all the layerings of *The Unforgettable Fire* wouldn't have worked if Clayton and Mullen hadn't found the target. The bass is subliminal, the drum sound isn't martially charged. They no longer intrude, instead they flow just beneath the surface of the new U2 sound. Discovering that pulse was equally crucial for the band's future.

There was another significant change: their artistic conscience was no longer tethered by the rigid demands of the Shalom sect. Now Bono could follow his intuition unchafed by the chains of false responsibility. *The Unforgettable Fire* was a spiritual album but it was allusive and inclusive. Touring America and watching its intolerant televangelists, U2 had now realised that moral exclusion zones patrolled by the self-righteous could kill the spirit. Insofar as the album is Christian, the Holy Ghost is the presiding member of the Trinity.

Bono also needed room for personal manoeuvre. As the live lightning conductor of the band, he'd become a sitting target for charges of self-righteousness, self-importance and melodrama. But with *The Unforgettable Fire*, U2 obviously weren't writing in tabloid headlines; its mystery would let Bono escape in the fog.

*The Unforgettable Fire* also found them switching from Windmill. They were dissatisfied with its room which was soon to be redesigned, so Eno introduced them to the opportunities of the portable studio which they installed at Slane Castle, the home of Lord Henry Mountcharles. The atmosphere was surreal. The generator that powered the studio often broke down. According to one of their technicians, Steve Rainford: 'Most of Edge's guitar was recorded with his amplifier outside on the balcony with a plastic bag over it so the rain wouldn't get in.'

Much of the album would later be recast during a second set of sessions at Windmill but the rural setting of Slane, beside the river Boyne, definitely contributed to the less frenetic, autumnal atmosphere of the album. And yet they still had a deadline crisis. Twelve days before the official finishing date with the band committed to an Australian tour, Bono told his partners he couldn't finish the lyrics. But they ploughed on, working 20-hour days for the final two weeks.

*The Unforgettable Fire* doesn't always work; there are a few moments when the Eno/Lanois production gloss dresses up Irish mutton as lamb. But both the title track and 'A Sort Of Homecoming' pointed the way to a new Eighties progressive-rock where European melodies could be blended with rock rhythms without sounding either alien, contrived or bloated techno-pomp.

And yet as with every U2 album, it also anticipates their next move. *The Unforgettable Fire* may have been their most 'European' record but it also introduces Bono's fascination with such American icons as Martin Luther King and Elvis Presley while 'Pride (In The Name Of Love)' was their most effective and concentrated piece of Top 40 songwriting so far.

---

## A SORT OF HOMECOMING

U2'S CHANGE is immediate from the first bar. Instead of marching in with a shout, the drums slap and bounce in with a polyrhythmic shuffle. The second switch and sign of Eno's influence is in the guitar, palpable but somehow entwined and almost buried in the mix with Bono's vocals and a repeated bass pattern leading the melody. For some time, Eno had bee ' challenging the conventional notions of 'ranking' instruments which always headlined the guitar. With this mix, the hierarchy is overturned; the old U2 sound is transformed into an instrumental dub.

The title comes from the cryptic, mystical German/Rumanian Jewish poet, Paul Celan, who drowned himself in the Seine in 1970 and who wrote 'poetry is a sort of homecoming'. A poet of pained yet most profound spiritual doubt, Celan contrasts with the band's earlier religious certainties.

So now the band enter the shadowlands. 'Your earth moves beneath your own dream landscape' could be the best introduction to this album's many twilight zones. But if the musical atmosphere is a flickering twilight, the lyrics are about transient experience, archetypes not dogma. 'On the borderlands we run... and don't look back' sings Bono. Already he's celebrating rather than being confused by contradictions; relaxed, no longer insecure about living on those borders and putting his faith in the quest itself.

## PRIDE
## (IN THE NAME OF LOVE)

THE FIRST release and hit single off the album, 'Pride...' was worked up from an idea conceived at a Hawaii sound check the previous November and then polished to perfection in the Windmill sessions. Apparently U2's most conventional 'rock' song yet, its secrets lie with Edge. It is his most virtuoso performance so far in the band's career – after the clarion intro, he continually varies the guitar pattern through each verse, chorus and melody, never exactly repeating the same riff once.

The lyrics hymn Martin Luther King, a man of peace and non-violent protest, an apt hero for four Irishmen, grappling to find a new way apart from the religious prejudice and violence of the North. And one secret revealed. The sleeve notes offer special thanks to Mrs. Christine Kerr a.k.a. Chrissie Hynde. The reason – visiting Dublin with The Pretenders, she came down to the studio to join Bono and Eno,

leading the 'Uh-Uh-Uh' backing vocals.

## WIRE

THE EDGE opens a new front with a guitar intro that could have been culled from African music. But though it's easy to point to Eno's work with Talking Heads, the influences are fully digested and used to the advantage of U2's own sound. Compare with 'Refugee' from *War*. When Edge plays his own variations on funk rhythm guitar, Adam and Larry are no longer distractions. Instead the music fuses and swells on the first anti-drug, pro-life song of the album.

## THE UNFORGETTABLE FIRE

ANOTHER abrupt shift as U2 again dump the guitar trio sound. Edge throws up a few flares at the start but the melody is really led by keyboards and then embellished by a string arrangement from Noel Kelehan, best known outside Ireland for conducting the RTE Orchestra in the Eurovision Song Contest.

The original 'Unforgettable Fire' and the alleged inspiration for the song was a travelling Japanese exhibition to commemorate the victims of Hiroshima, that the band attended in Chicago. Even so, Bono's lyrics are so widely open to interpretation that they hardly seem an obvious anti-nuclear lament. Like much of the album, they're more a travelogue of the soul, a journey from where 'city lights shine in silver and gold' onto a 'carnival – the wheels fly and colours spin' onto a mysterious encounter 'face to face in a dry and waterless place'.

Besides, the music's surging exhilaration hardly expresses grim tragedy. It's not so much what Bono's singing but how. Steve Lillywhite tended to patch in vocal parts from different performances whereas Eno went for the complete take and Bono was now starting to cruise on the melody rather than choke on the emotion.

Seeking literal meaning can be a waste of time since Bono's allowed free association according to his own inarticulate speech of the heart. Again spiritual aspiration seems to be the guiding emotion but it can also be heard as a love song.

## PROMENADE

CAN BE heard as Bono's own sort of homecoming to Bray, 'the slide-show seaside town' just south of Dublin with its own promenade. There he lived with his wife, Alison, in a redesigned Martello tower with its own 'spiral staircase to the higher ground' overlooking the local 'football ground' of Bray Wanderers. The bedroom on the top floor had a glass roof, so take the music as starlit memories.

## 4TH OF JULY

A SKETCH that seems to drift in from nowhere, the story goes that this was an unintentional instrumental. Eno eavesdropped on Edge and Adam fooling around and recorded, treated and mixed it without the pair knowing. Certainly this is an example of 'the lyrical soul in abundance', which Eno believed U2 had wrongly feared and repressed. He'd brought back the band of 'An Cat Dubh'/'Into The Heart' and 'October'.

## BAD

LIKE 'WIRE', a plea to a junkie. As in many UK cities, the Eighties recession had led to an unprecedented rise in inner city heroin casualties in Dublin. British indie bands of the era were now starting to blend the Velvets and The Byrds but Edge's foundation riff strays down a different if parallel track with echoes of both Lou Reed's 'Walk On The Wild Side' and Van Morrison's 'Astral Weeks'.

It's a slight but significant difference; he loses little in tone but definitely gains in the droning insistent rhythm that would make 'Bad' U2's ultimate show-stealer live. Bono's performance almost contrasts the two worlds of Reed and Morrison, between 'the lifeless lifeline' of junk and the man who's 'wide awake... not sleeping'. Then there's the famous, even notorious sequence of seven '-ation' rhymes, U2 and Bono's proof that rock need not always bother about literal meaning, that it's about how something is expressed not what is expressed.

## INDIAN SUMMER SKY

IF 'WIRE' digests Eno's Talking Heads experiences, this is the album's one derivative track where U2 don't quite master its two obvious D.B. influences from Messrs. Byrne and Bowie. One can't fault individual performances – the guitar flickers brightly, the rhythm pair are fluent and Bono again shows the new composure in his singing – but the vocal refrain, 'So wind go through to my heart' must have sent many listeners off to check the Heads' 'Remain In Light'.

## ELVIS PRESLEY IN AMERICA

THE SECOND track that came from a trickster Eno experiment. He'd slowed down the basic rhythm track of 'A Sort Of Homecoming' (a clue for those who've got a turntable and a vinyl version, play this at 45 and compare Larry's drum patterns), encouraged Bono to improvise at the mike and then told the surprised singer it was a wrap. 'Like watching a dress-rehearsal from off-stage,' commented Edge later as Bono moans and mumbles his meditations on Presley.

This was and often still is how Bono composes his lyrics, fumbling through some private communion . 'Tell me how to sing,' he pleads, later confiding 'no one taught you how but you knew the King knows how to howl' before wailing wordlessly off into some Pentecostalist fog. It shouldn't work but somehow Bono sustains the emotion and makes you believe the spirit is with him. Elvis has just entered U2's building for the first time.

## MLK

AS ALSO Martin Luther King for the second time. Just a cloud-bank of synths but 'MLK' is a companion to 'October', a healing song of faith not a lament over the grave. 'If the thundercloud passes rain, so let it rain, let it rain, rain on you.' A principle had been established by '40': however cathartic U2's music might be, they would always close with a mood of healing and hope. After the album was finished, Eno argued there were '4 or 5 U2's on it'. The last two tracks might have been taken as a hint that some of those new U2's were now heading back to America.

# The Joshua Tree

Island U26; released March 1987

**T**HE **U**NFORGETTABLE **F**IRE **HAD PRIMED PEOPLE TO EXPECT THE UNEXPECTED** from U2 and *The Joshua Tree*, delivered after a 30-month gap, again found them confounding predictions. Where *The Unforgettable Fire* sprawled and veered off into the realms of the unconscious, *The Joshua Tree* was concise and often as politically specific as U2 would ever get. If *The Unforgettable Fire* was an album of breadth, pushing the boundaries, *The Joshua Tree* was an album of depth, working within the constraining disciplines of the song.

Much had happened to the band during those two years and more. *Time* magazine would soon call them 'rock's hottest ticket'. Their show-stealing performance of 'Bad' at Live Aid meant U2 had ceased to be the secret and private property of their fans. Rock's biggest underground band had exploded overground and, as a result, they'd starred on Amnesty's Conspiracy Of Hope tour. It's entirely possible they would have already entered the megastar bracket if *The Unforgettable Fire* had contained a couple of other radio-friendly singles to follow 'Pride (In The Name Of Love)'.

Meanwhile they were still hungry for new ideas and experiences with Bono to the fore. With his wife, Ali, he'd volunteered for charity work in Ethiopia – the only Band Aid and Live Aid participant besides Bob Geldof to actively investigate what was happening there. He was also exploring areas of music that had not previously interested him.

Bob Dylan was one catalyst. When Dylan had played Slane Castle in 1984, Bono had guested on an encore and then talked with him and Van Morrison for an informal *Hot Press* interview. This relationship with Dylan would develop. Some months later, I met Bono in a Dublin night-club and he went home early in the morning to receive a phone call from Dylan. But then U2 and Bono especially were always the sons who wanted to learn from the wisdom of the fathers; they'd already struck up chummy relationships with Bruce Springsteen and Pete Townshend.

At their first meeting, Dylan had disorientated Bono by talking about his own debt to Irish music and especially The Clancy Brothers, the prototype Irish ballad group who'd played Greenwich Village in Dylan's early folk days. Till then, U2, with the partial exception of their country and Elvis fan, Larry Mullen, hadn't been much interested in any Irish or American roots music.

Like all the young bands of their generation, they'd reacted against the prevailing Irish trends of the Seventies. From their perspective, Irish music seemed archaic, too nationalist and an obstacle to new ideas. In their early days, they'd also been rightly unimpressed by the clichéd blooze-rock bar-bands then littering the Dublin scene. But now Bono entered a phase where he would duet with Clannad on 'In A Lifetime', write 'Silver And Gold' and recruit Keith Richards and Ronnie Wood to perform it for Little Steven's Sun City project.

The band from the South of Ireland would now dive into the American Deep South. The experience would teach Bono how to explore and reconcile the divide between the secular and the spiritual in his soul. Blues and rock'n'roll too often used Biblical imagery and Bono's reading would also now turn to American literature with Flannery O'Connor a particular favourite. In consequence, his lyrics would become far less vague and he would start to write in narrative idioms.

They would also understand better how to relate Christianity to social justice. Outsiders still often related Christianity to the reactionary televangelists of the Moral Majority but U2 would find an escape from that trap. Touring for Amnesty and through Bono's travels in Ethiopia and Central America, they would encounter the radical Christian and Catholic aid charities dealing with poverty and oppression in the Third World.

Again, this was a particularly Irish response. *Per capita*, the Republic had been by far the largest contributor of donations to Live Aid. In response to the Troubles in the North, much Southern political and religious idealism had been deflected into Third World relief agencies like Concern. *The Joshua Tree* would be the one album by a major act that even noticed, let alone started to investigate, the larger and more painful issues surrounding Live Aid.

They were already signalling their changes before the album was released. In January 1986, they premièred an intentionally rough version of 'Trip Through Your Wires' on RTE's *T.V. Gaga* show. Their short Conspiracy Of Hope set was débuted at the Dublin Self Aid show in May and included Eddie Cochran's 'C'Mon Everybody' and a vicious version of Dylan's 'Maggie's Farm'.

But none of this would have mattered if they hadn't mastered the art of songwriting. Methods changed. Previously U2 material was usually worked out at band jams; now Bono and Edge often brought basic song ideas to Adam and Larry. With Nineties hindsight, it can all seem funny peculiar. Only on their fifth album, into their second contract, had U2 learned proper joined-up songwriting. Could any act expect such a long and lucrative apprenticeship now?

But other working methods remained unchanged. Again Lanois and Eno produced, though the Canadian now took a more influential role. Again much work occurred outside the studio, this time with an Amek console at Edge's and Adam's houses.

The original band was still detectable on tracks like 'Where The Streets

Have No Name' and 'In God's Country' but they'd shed their first skin. U2 now underplayed and left spaces; Edge was no longer required to layer overdubbed curtains of sound to fill every gap.

Indeed it's remarkable how easily they slipped into their new identity. The album skilfully pastiches a variety of Top 40 Rock styles of the time. There's hints of Police and Lou Reed, traces of Rod Stewart in the rock ballads, and Jimi Hendrix and Led Zeppelin enter their vocabulary for the first time on 'Bullet The Blue Sky'. Dylan too is a new presence palpable on 'Trip Through Your Wires'. Yet their own distinctive voice wasn't drowned out by their borrowings. *The Joshua Tree* is unmistakably classic U2 since these new influences release rather than imprison the band.

And then on the second side, when listeners might have been starting to suspect U2 were getting too radio-friendly, they strike out again in new directions. With the gorgeous World Music lilt of 'One Tree Hill' and then, crucially, with the savage 'Exit'. This was a key song in their future development since now it seems so obviously the first ancestor of the jagged sound and songs of bleak spiritual doubt on *Achtung Baby*.

For some time, Bono had been speaking of his ambition to make a record with all the diversity of The Beatles' *White Album*. This album lacks the sprawling anarchy of The Beatles' record but it's the first conclusive evidence that the best young live band of their era had graduated as masterful pop mimics in the studio. With *The Joshua Tree*, their recorded work finally catches up and even outstrips their live reputation.

Bono is one major reason. Beforehand, while he might dominate on stage, he didn't always focus on record, especially since he was often a laggard struggling with the lyrics. But on *The Joshua Tree*, he knew his themes and targets. His lyrics leave the dreamtime for often harsh, daylight realities. This extra substance in the songs led to a new emotional authority and accuracy in his singing.

This individual and collective evolution between albums also shows how and why U2 have endured as a creative as well as a commercial force. Round about 1987, the Second British Invasion began to peter out. Its acts either fell foul of lifestyle problems or produced soundalike albums or records whose attempted change of direction was unconvincing. Till then U2 had often been associated with a pack of Big Music bands, notably Simple Minds, The Waterboys, Big Country and a very reluctant Echo & The Bunnymen. With *The Joshua Tree*, incidentally the first platinum million-selling CD in America, U2 launched themselves into their own solitary stratosphere.

They'd also won because they were still refusenik romantics, the last gang in town who still believed that rock shouldn't limit its horizons to private pleasures and problems. U2 didn't want rock to be a lifestyle accessory; they still insisted it might just involve some public dimension, some raising of communal consciousness. Despite the Reagan years, there were still some optimists who shared those beliefs.

However, let's not exaggerate the idealism in their audience. The hit singles and their new welcome into Top 40 radio also won them another new audience of Young American teens who weren't necessarily appreciating them for their philosophy.

Really U2 had been surfing a wave since Live Aid. As so often happens, a band can seize their time. Their Irish optimism, curiosity and adaptability gave them a special empathy with America, while their humanism tuned into a new generosity. But equally importantly, the chance for their breakthrough arrived just as their recording and songwriting skills reached maturity.

*The Joshua Tree* was the summarising symbol of the album. It was the name of the Californian desert town where Gram Parsons went drinking and fixin' to die; it's also the name of the desert's most resilient cactus. Even in the worst drought, life and the waters of salvation could still be found.

The album sleeve caused some ambivalence. Were these Irishmen in their cowboy clobber Mexican emigrants or lost gringos? Were they play-acting in a spaghetti Western or some more serious drama? And had the Irish the right to plunder and play with American images and music? In the aftermath of this album, those questions would hit U2 in the solar plexus.

---

## WHERE THE STREETS HAVE NO NAME

FOR THE opening track, the band fed their fans' sense of anticipation with a slowly swelling keyboard intro over which Edge, Adam and Larry set a frantic, soaring tone for no less than one minute 46 seconds before Bono arrives. With Edge's skittering guitar, the first track is familiar U2 though the mood's far more sunlit than the autumnal weather of *The Unforgettable Fire*. But where were those 'streets with no name'? There were two usual answers: the streets of both America's cities and the derelict, abandoned ghost towns of the desert. It could also be a refer-ence to the cities and towns of high-land Ethiopia where streets are also numbered, not named. You don't write lines like 'Show you a place/High on a desert plain/Where the streets have no name' about the canyons of Manhattan.

## I STILL HAVEN'T FOUND WHAT I'M LOOKING FOR

THE FIRST song that shows what a leap U2 (and Bono) had made. From one superficial perspective, it's a smart job of pop hackwork, pretty standard American radio rock-ballad fare with the appropri-ate degree of uplift in the chorus to inspire the Yanks. But it's far more than just another stadium rabble-rouser to be played during the breaks in American football matches. The band's rhythms are far more supple and cultivated than your average bouffant HM band of that period; there's a spring and bounce in Larry Mullen's offbeats which those whitebread bands never played. Again U2's Island background gave their music an extra flavour.

Besides, its religious theme hardly suited a half-time anthem. On *The Unforgettable Fire*, Bono had moved beyond dogma to explore the quest for faith, but here he isn't hiding behind codes, metaphors or Brian Eno's cloudy production but had fashioned a spiritual song that even agnostics could admire.

Faith becomes not an act of blind obedience and death-delivering dogma – I don't believe this song could have been written by an Irish Catholic, lapsed or otherwise – but a constant struggle, with hope the ally in the search for renewal. In other hands, its themes could have been black and pessimistic but the melody and performance of 'I Still Haven't Found What I'm Looking For' are free from despair and welcome the spiritual challenge ahead.

Moreover Bono's witness – 'I believe in the kingdom come/And all the colours bleed into one' – was inclusive not exclusive. Not surprisingly, it appealed to Americans' own restless and shape-shifting religiosity.

## WITH OR WITHOUT YOU

A MASTERFUL pop song that reveals how U2 had learned the lessons of emotional restraint. Bass and drums pad in and what sounds like keyboards is Edge unfurling his Infinite guitar, a gizmo invented by Michael Brook with whom he'd worked on the *Captive* soundtrack. Again Bono's theme of self-surrender is familiar but his vocals are measured, no longer hurtling over the brink. Likewise the band now had the emotional experience and technical expertise to build a performance. Now they simmered and the kettle didn't squeal.

Like 'I Still Haven't Found...' it's also proof that U2 had reinvented themselves as a quality pop band. The basic design might have come from Sting's bottom drawer but here U2 had taken a contemporary and familiar style and invested it with their own character.

In another sense, this is also U2's first real adult love song. Being both 'with or without you' are equally tormented emotional states. As the song unfolds, there's tension and a quality of detachment and deliberation in the early verses – 'a bed of nails/she makes me wait' – which makes the catharsis of the later choruses far more intense. 'And you *give* and you *give* and you give yourself away', Bono sings, caught in that peculiarly suspended state of ego loss where love can dissolve the sense of self. Somehow I could never quite understand why he was so regularly accused of egotism when so many of his lyrics concern ego*less*ness.

It's tender and, above all, vulnerable. 'She's got me with nothing to win and nothing left to lose' he sings before the final chorus, and the restraint is underscored by the final instrumental reprise. Other bands might have climaxed with a romantic storm but U2 instead close with the calm after.

## BULLET THE BLUE SKY

VERY SIMPLY put, 'Bullet...' was the result of two discoveries. Edge found Jimi Hendrix and Bono experienced the Central American conflict when he travelled to San Salvador and Nicaragua through the good offices of Amnesty International. With it, the album moves from personal to political themes and Bono has always claimed the song was inspired by an incident in San Salvador when he witnessed government planes attacking a band of peasants.

Again the Irish context is important. The Nicaraguan and the other Central American conflicts received far more coverage in Ireland than in Britain. The Irish identified with the Nicaraguans who they believed were being bullied by the larger power of America. Many radical Catholic missionaries served in Central America and the since discredited Bishop Casey was present at the mass where El Salvador's Archbishop Romero was killed by government forces. Some

years later, Nicaragua's rebel President Daniel Ortega would visit Ireland and meet U2, a private and then unpublicised encounter set up by Michael D. Higgins, Ireland's Arts Minister since 1993. There is a further Irish link in that Amnesty's American chapter was led by Jack Healey, an Irish-American who formerly a Franciscan priest.

But the track also dramatises an internal conflict between the US's own angels and demons. The ugly Americans 'peeling off those dollar bills' were the agents of religious imperialism, the fundamental sects who influenced the conservative forces in the region, and Bono's lyrics contrast the burning crosses of the Klu Klux Klan with the liberating spirit of the John Coltrane of 'A Love Supreme', the man who 'breathes into a saxophone'. Ultimately the song pivots on its ambiguous final line. 'Outside is America' but which face is it showing? With 'Bullet...' , U2 had learned they must deal with both the promise and the threat.

U2 had sometimes flirted with hard rock but they'd always been wary lest they be trapped by its formulas. But on 'Bullet...' they sidestepped its pitfalls. Edge went back to the music's more enterprising Sixties origins in the styles of The Who, Led Zeppelin and especially Jimi Hendrix when all the feedback furies usually served a tune not a laboured riff, and the music hadn't completely lost the flavour of the blues.

Again 'Bullet...' distanced U2

U2 in early 1981. Left to right: Adam Clayton, Bono,
The Edge and Larry Mullen Jnr.

The young U2 on the streets of Dublin.

Peter Rowan, six-year-old younger
brother of Bono's friend Guggi
(Derek Rowan), of The Virgin
Prunes, on the cover of the *Boy*
album, released in 1980.

*October*, released in October, 1981.

Clockwise, from top left: Larry, Bono, Adam & The Edge.

Top: Peter Rowan graces a U2 sleeve for the second time, on *War* (1983); and, below, *Under A Blood Red Sky*, recorded at various shows during 1983.

Bono on stage, his confidence growing by the time of *War*.

Top: *The Unforgettable Fire*, released in October 1984; and, below, *Wide Awake In America*, featuring the explosive live version of 'Bad'.

The Edge on stage.

*The Joshua Tree*, the album that turned U2 into superstars, released in 1987.

Bono on stage during the 'Joshua Tree' tour, 1987.

Backstage during the 'Lovetown' tour, 1989

Bono on stage during the 'Lovetown' tour.

*Rattle And Hum* (1988) and *Achtung Baby* (1991)

Bono in 'Zoo TV' guise, 1992.

from their British Big Music contemporaries and showed they were capable of a far wider range of styles. And just as The Smiths were emerging with Johnny Marr inaugurating a new school of guitar-playing that deleted Keith Richard and The Clash in favour of The Velvets and The Byrds, Edge was travelling against the tide of the new fashion. But it made sense. Any guitarist who married rhythm and melody like Edge was destined to tangle with rhythm'n'blues playing and the legacy of Hendrix.

But if 'Bullet...' broke new ground, it's also a blueprint since the version is superseded by the epic live performance developed for *Rattle And Hum*.

## RUNNING TO STAND STILL

THE FINAL and fifth track on what was easily U2's best vinyl side to date. 'Running To Stand Still' remains their finest Dublin anthem, returning to the 'seven towers' of Ballymun, the housing development close to Bono's home that was also the site of Roddy Doyle's TV drama series, *Family*.

There, heroin had become the other escape route from the one U2 had been sufficiently lucky and talented to take. But if this ballad is suitably mournful it's also flecked by an uncannily sympathetic compassion that refuses to cast stones at the woman who's the victim of junk. Heroin too can be a temporary transcendence but the meaning of the melody is that there are other

rivers to take out of hopelessness.

Appropriately the music takes a lead from the Lou Reed songbook but there's also a trace element of Van Morrison and shades of the Bruce Springsteen of *Nebraska* in Bono's keening and harmonica playing. And yet again U2 show their new versatility since the essentially acoustic performance is basically dominated by Bono and Edge with Larry Mullen taking only a brief cameo drum part.

## RED HILL MINING TOWN

HERE THE original vinyl version turned over to a far more disparate second side. 'Red Hill Mining Town' is the album's third ballad but it contrasts with both 'I Still Haven't Found' and 'Running To Stand Still' in that it's the most cluttered and literal, least mysterious and open-ended track on the album. The blocked harmonies on the chorus give the impression of a band striving too ambitiously and conventionally for effect. Their detractors wouldn't be completely out of order if they deemed it a scarf-waving variant of 'Sailing' written for the National Union of Mineworkers.

A pity they miscalculated since the melody is undeniably potent and infectious. Furthermore the song was born from fine intentions, a meditation on the social wreckage caused by the attack on mining communities that left so many unemployed and with uncertain futures.

It was the song on the album

least played live. One can only wonder how it might have developed if they'd filleted its excess weight.

## IN GOD'S COUNTRY

THE ALBUM'S second return to a more standard and familiar U2, 'In God's Country' is probably most significant as the last song U2 recorded in their original trademark style. And even here Adam's rumbling counterpoint bass figure before Edge's guitar break is a mark of their progress.

It's also a companion piece to 'Where The Streets Have No Name' since Bono's back in the desert again, though this time the emotional landscape of 'sad eyes, crooked crosses' is more identifiably American. But really, this is U2 cruising, a starter not a main course. And though Bono's lyrics are clichés, they're saved by the fact that he did Bono better than anybody else.

## TRIP THROUGH YOUR WIRES

DÉBUTED ON RTE as a throwaway, 'Trip Through Your Wires' was intended to present a new informal U2, a band of buskers who were now supping from the same brew as Dylan, the new folk-friendly Waterboys and The Hot House Flowers. But the studio version is indecisive. U2 seem uncertain whether to opt for carefree spontaneity or develop the song's basic idea and the combination of Adam's foursquare bass and Larry's packing-case Glitter Band drums

doesn't embellish it much either.

Bono's dualism about women as angels or devils re-emerges but can be accepted in the context of 'Trip Through Your Wires' as an unsteady, stumbling drinker's song. His harp's fun too but this was a far more convincing carouse in its later live version.

## ONE TREE HILL

THIS WAS dedicated to the memory of Greg Carroll, a New Zealand Maori who'd worked hardly a year as Bono's personal assistant. Taking Bono's bike to run an errand on a rain swept Dublin night, he crashed into a car and was killed instantly. Happening just as the band were starting to record the album, the death of Greg Carroll, who'd speedily become a much-loved member of the team, was a shattering experience for U2 and their close-knit organisation.

They gave him a celebration not a lament. Edge found a loose-limbed guitar melody with both an African and a Hawaiian tinge and the surge of the playing and Bono's imagery fused to recapture Greg Carroll's sea-going Maori heritage. Furthermore the lyrics, with their reference to traditional Maori burial ceremonies on One Tree Hill, indicated that the band's faith didn't exclude an empathy with others' beliefs and rituals. Their Christianity wouldn't plaster over the universal archetypes of mourning.

And yet despite its moving vocal coda, 'One Tree Hill' isn't sombre. It celebrates the life of the spirit not its extinction. Greg Carroll would not be diminished in death.

## EXIT

FOR ANYONE who was really listening, 'Exit' should have exploded the myth of U2 as the nice guys of rock. Never had they shown such a vicious streak or produced such a withering track. Edge's sheets of sound return but now they're not glistening but gorged with anger. Far more than even 'Bullet The Blue Sky', his playing is scratching at the prison bars of polished good taste.

But then, up till this track, U2 had preached alternatives to violence and evil; their music preferred to be inspirational not confrontational and had never really wrestled with those beasts in the bottommost pit. But 'Exit', the wildest card in *The Joshua Tree*, is both a complete reversal of their previous public artistic character and a crucial clue to their later development that many missed.

Around this time, I remember Bono talking about another Dublin rock singer, Simon Carmody of The Golden Horde. Carmody had the violence all singers needed but did he, wondered Bono, have the understanding to channel it? Certainly on 'Exit', Bono the singer ceased being afraid of calling up his own furies, dramatising that fanaticism where dogmatism verges with psychosis and a man will go 'deeper into black, deeper into white' and kill with 'the hands of love'.

For the first time, he was owning up to the dangers of the dualism implicit in Christianity. The track's also notable as the first time U2 strayed onto the ground previously monopolised by their Lypton Village associates, The Virgin Prunes. The similarities aren't only spiritual. Edge's elder brother, Dik, very briefly an early member of U2, also played a far more scalding and discordantly feedback-drenched guitar style with the Prunes.

But again only a committed believer could have got inside the skull of the protagonist of 'Exit'. On the succeeding tour, performances of 'Exit' would grow ever more fraught and purgative. A year later, an American accused of murder would claim the song drove him to that drastic deed.

## MOTHERS OF THE DISAPPEARED

THE JOSHUA Tree is easily U2's most global album with Bono, the band's foreign correspondent on assignment in Ethiopia, Central America and New Zealand. Now their Amnesty contacts supplied them with an Argentinean theme for the closing track.

Through the Seventies and until the middle of the Eighties, the Argentinean military junta had arrested many of its student opponents who were never seen again, dead or alive. An organisation of the bereaved, literally called Mothers Of The Disappeared, was formed. When democracy returned in the wake of the disastrous Falklands/ Malvinas war with Britain, they campaigned for the disclosure of the full truth and the trial of those who had kidnapped, tortured and killed their children.

The track continued the tradition of '40' and 'MLK', for how long would the Mothers of the Disappeared sing their song? Again the lament works on a drone with Bono testifying 'we hear their heartbeats'. But its intro with Eno's percussive treatment of a piano is more experimental and the shadows of this lament are punctuated by a barbed guitar interjection.

# Rattle And Hum

Island U27; released October 1988

**R**ATTLE AND HUM **IS EASILY U2'S MOST CONTROVERSIAL ALBUM. IT WAS A** commercial success, selling over 14 million copies but never did U2 receive such critical dog's abuse for a record.

The old charges of self-importance re-emerged. U2 were seen to be making the album of the movie of the book of the world domination campaign. Even more heinously, they were misappropriating icons like Elvis Presley and B. B. King to boost their status. If U2 claimed they were merely paying the reverent homage of humble fans, their detractors insisted they were guilty of the sin of pride, blasphemously elevating themselves into the pantheon of rock gods. Another school of thought, especially prominent in England, accused them of a regressive infatuation with outmoded rock'n'roll. The new arena stars had made the backward mistake of mutating into mouldy old pub-rockers.

Later U2 would concede that when they planned the film, they misplanned the record. It had initially been intended as a scrapbook album, a set of postcards from America but this casual approach conflicted with the hype that inevitably surrounded the movie. The overall *Rattle And Hum* project became the victim of such contradictions.

More than any previous U2 project, *Rattle And Hum* was Bono's album. All its triumphs, errors and superficial scrappiness flow from him and it sometimes seems as if the other three are tidying up his action-painting. If *Rattle And Hum* bravely tests both the limits of stardom and the live album, it was also inevitable that the future Fly was sometimes going to buzz and blunder into the window-pane.

The band's adoption of America also rankled. Yet as Irishmen, U2 had ducked out of the TransAtlantic rock and cultural civil war between Britain and America. Historically the States had always been a welcoming land of opportunity for the Irish. Musically and culturally, there were many natural links between the Southern states and Ireland with Irish traditional music the root of bluegrass and country. And during the tour, they'd also made a habit of dressing up and performing as The Dalton Brothers, a caricature country band.

Besides, after touring America for seven years, U2 felt they had to give witness to their experiences. The clash between sex and religion, most pronounced in the Southern states, fascinated all of them, especially Bono, who was also fixated by the gospel spirit of black music. An album like *Rattle And Hum* was probably inevitable. The real question is whether *Rattle And Hum* was the best expression of these themes.

At points, it can seem too didactic. Critics, though, forgot that through *The Joshua Tree* U2 had won a new and younger pop audience who knew very little about such great American national treasures like B. B. King or Sun Records. And if U2's enthusiasm can seem overbearing – 'Eat your greens, eat your blues, they're good for you' – well, they'd usually preferred the populist approach to élitist cool.

They'd also taken a particularly Irish route into America. U2 were almost Irish folkies, excavating musical history to find the common hidden seams between Ireland and America.

*Rattle And Hum* was more post-modernist in its confusions and surprise discoveries than its initial musical intentions. Rap and black music's post-soul agenda are absent. If Martin Luther King is one of the album's presiding spirits, they hadn't even decided how to learn to cope with the legacy of Malcolm X.

Double-albums had also become rare by 1988 and the patchwork nature of the record didn't encourage a friendly critical response. On early hearings, the flippant and the intense, live and studio tracks, seemed carelessly scattered together without any unifying theme. The band's throwaway versions of 'All Along The Watchtower' and The Beatles' 'Helter Skelter' got the most stick yet new songs like 'Hawkmoon 269', 'God Part II' and 'All I Want Is You' were as good if not better than anything they'd previously recorded.

*Rattle And Hum* might have been better received if they'd separated the live from the studio cuts. But they didn't take that option. Instead, they sequenced the album to follow the soundtrack of the movie.

The recording of the album was also different from anything they'd ever done. 'Heartland' was a leftover from earlier sessions with Eno and Lanois but the other studio tracks were recorded on the run, either in America or STS, a small Dublin studio in the city's Temple Bar area they used for their demos. And, with American material, they used an American producer, Jimmy Iovine, brought back after working on *Under A Blood Red*

*Sky*. A New Yorker who'd served his apprenticeship working with John Lennon and Bruce Springsteen, Iovine gave the album a more compressed and directly dramatic feel.

*Rattle And Hum* also documents their immediate and contradictory responses to the megastardom they'd attained through *The Joshua Tree*. The film was meant to consolidate that status but the album is a far more unruly affair, intended as a diary of their emotions and experiences that uses music almost to escape and offload the strain. Bono is uncertain how to comment on his own stardom, so on 'God Part II', he deflects it into a blast at Albert Goldman's muckraking biography of John Lennon.

*Rattle And Hum* also showed a different side of America from *The Joshua Tree*. It attacked American power while *Rattle And Hum* celebrated American popular culture, those American Dreams we have happily allowed to colonise our consciousness. And one is definitely opposed to the other. The spirits invoked on *Rattle And Hum* are definitely summoned to exorcise the demons of *The Joshua Tree*.

But the curiosity was that, unlike many before and since, U2 didn't fumble the opportunity. The orchestra of The Unforgettable Fire now had the versatility to master more traditional forms on 'Desire', 'Angel Of Harlem' and 'When Love Comes To Town'. Few bands had shown such songwriting scope.

*Rattle And Hum* was a sprawling mongrel of an album, flawed both by under- and over-ambition. But those who signed on for the trip found that it contained some of U2's greatest moments.

---

## HELTER SKELTER

'NOBODY told us there'd be days like this' – John Lennon's rueful line about the chaos when stardom suddenly strikes – as quoted to me by Bono in a *Hot Press* interview during the last leg of the tour. This opening live track – recorded like most of the live material at Denver's McNichols Arena on November 8 for the black'n'white section of the film – was misinterpreted as if U2 were blaspheming and claiming to be the new Fab Four whereas this choice of a Beatles cover was really intended as the album's preface, reflecting all the confusion of the tour and their new superstar status. But Bono's opening line – 'Charles Manson stole this song from The Beatles, we're stealing it back' – hardly helped their case. In effect, it was his Christian conscience speaking, but this efficient performance needed rather more wildness if the song was to be wrestled back from Mr. Manson's grasp.

## VAN DIEMAN'S LAND

FURTHER confusion. Nobody could have expected Edge with just a naked arpeggio-plucked guitar singing a 19th Century ballad about an Irish felon shipped to Australia. The song was inspired by one John Boyle O'Reilly, a leader of the desperate 1848 Rising against the Crown that followed the Great Famine. After all, it was enforced emigration that brought Irish music to both Australia and America. Over a hundred years later, Rattle And Hum, albeit without any coercion, follows those footsteps. But yet again, this is not a rebel song that makes past oppression an excuse for violence as the last verse – 'Still the gunman rules and widows pay/A scarlet coat now a black beret' – makes clear.

## DESIRE

THE REAL deal starts here. Recorded at Dublin's STS studio, U2 make their latest chameleon change and nail down a staple of American traditional music, the Bo Diddley beat, though Edge would later claim the track was based on a reworking of a Stooges riff, '1969' to be precise. Bono sings 'I'm like a preacher/Stealing hearts at a travelling show/For love or money, money?', an early hint of his role-playing on Zoo TV. Larry Mullen gets to reveal himself as a true rock'n'roll drummer, a Sixties pop organ provides a dollop of Las Vegas sauce and U2 prove their versatility by mastering the throwaway single.

## HAWKMOON 269

THE TEMPERATURE continues to rise on this thunderous track. Bob Dylan dropped by to play organ but Jimmy Iovine's experiences with Spector and Lennon are the musical key. Alex Acuna's percussion and especially Larry Bunker's timpani combine with Larry Mullen's drumming for a monster rhythm track. With the title from a desert road sign, Bono launches into a litany of metaphors, each chant ending in the refrain, 'I need your love'. As the rhythms get even more extreme, Bono's out over some existential abyss, almost screaming at God-like David in the Psalms. Eventually the back-up trio, Edna Wright, Carolyn Wills and Billie Barnum ride in with a line unlisted in the lyric sheet – 'Meet all your love in the harlot'. Outside is America is Babylon.

## ALL ALONG THE WATCHTOWER

THE SECOND infamous cover to rile the sceptics, 'All Along The Watchtower' was cheekily busked at the free Save The Yuppie outdoor concert in San Francisco on November 8. Performed with a minimum of rehearsal, the casual informality is at odds with Bono's conviction and his claim: 'All I've got is a red guitar, three chords and the truth.' All mouth and no musical trousers? Well, by the later Lovetown tour, U2 had risen to a far more searing version of the song that, sadly, can only be found on bootlegs.

## I STILL HAVEN'T FOUND WHAT I'M LOOKING FOR/ FREEDOM FOR MY PEOPLE

AN OBJECT lesson in how the meaning of a song can be amplified in concert. Once U2 learned that 'I Still Haven't Found...' had been covered by a New Jersey gospel group, the New Voices Of Freedom, the opportunity for collaboration was just too tempting to miss. A majestic performance that is obviously and most audibly inspiring the Madison Square Garden audience, Bono shows his new authority as a singer by the fact that he isn't upstaged by the gospel choir and their two soloists, George Pendergrass and Dorothy Terrell.

Bono has written a thus far unrecorded song, 'The Three Kings Of Memphis' about Martin Luther King, Elvis Presley and B. B. King and here we meet all the fervour of the first. By recruiting the gospel choir, a song about spiritual doubts and desires enters a wider cultural arena. Most took stadium rock's notions of community from Woodstock but U2 were different – the monster meeting that ended the Civil Rights March on Washington was their touchstone. So this version transcends doubt and is instead a massive Pentecostalist yea-saying that taps into the sources and spirits of liberation. Giving witness is inevitably at odds with pop irony.

## SILVER AND GOLD

FROM Martin Luther King to Archbishop Desmond Tutu. The original appeared on the 'Artists Against Apartheid' album, organised by Little Steven, written by Bono on a brainstorming night immediately after he and his wife had returned from working at a World Vision camp in Ethiopia. And if U2 could never match the spontaneous intensity of the original, performed with Keith Richard and Ronnie Wood, there's still the sense of a band on the run, risking their credit to explore new ideas.

Bono's original lyric stole from Jesse Jackson – 'I am someone' – and Brendan Behan – 'I seen the coming and the going/*The captains and the kings*' – and locates both apartheid and the earlier enslavement of Africans in greed. Again his heated rap against Reagan's opposition to economic sanctions comes from a hunger to bear witness against apathy and the notion that rock is mere entertainment. But as with the opening Charles Manson remark, he got severe flak from his throwaway line, 'O.K. Edge, play the blues.'

## PRIDE (IN THE NAME OF LOVE)

THE OBVIOUS choice to complete this live triptych. Gospel music and the example of Martin Luther King had taught U2 that Christian religious belief and rock weren't necessarily irreconcilable enemies and led them into a totally unexplored area. But this is the most predictable live track on the album, a crowd-pleasing performance for the fans. The previous two performances stretch the originals. 'Pride' may bear testimony to the band's mastery of live performance but it reveals little new about U2, aside from their empathy with their audience.

## ANGEL OF HARLEM

FROM THE sacred to the profane on the other side of the Memphis tracks in Sun Studios where U2 hooked up with veteran country and rock'n'roll producer, Cowboy Jack Clement. Bono had definitely seized the reins and the song isn't only a tribute to Billie Holiday; it's also about a fan's experience in discovering the riches of American music and was as much about U2's voyage since four very gauche Irish teens had first landed at New York's Kennedy Airport over six years previously.

Now they were most adept magpies and mimics, comfortable writing and playing in any style. A personal favourite since it's the U2 song closest to Bono's enthusiasm and empathy as a night-owl conversationalist.

## LOVE RESCUE ME

WITHOUT doubt, the riskiest, because it's the most apparently regressive song on the album. This is almost U2's version of country'n'Irish, a country-soul ballad that could have been bawled out on any amateur night in a Northside Dublin pub. As far from *The Unforgettable Fire* as U2 could possibly get, its lyrics, co-written with Bob Dylan, are a mutual meditation on the stardom that had just struck Bono so fiercely on this tour. And yet while he's complaining 'Many lost who seek to find themselves in me/They ask me to reveal/The very thoughts they would conceal', he's still clinging to the hope of the title. The imagery is often biblical but the love sought is definitely not exclusive and sectarian.

And as so often with U2, move fast forward. As a song about spiritual quest, 'Love Rescue Me' is definitely an ancestor of 'The Wanderer', the Johnny Cash collaboration that closes *Zooropa*. As for Sun Studios, the ghost of Elvis Presley is definitely in the building and the song.

## WHEN LOVE COMES TO TOWN

BY THE END of recording *The Joshua Tree*, Bono was exploring the idea of writing songs for others. One candidate was Willie Nelson, another B. B. King, and just before *The Joshua Tree* was released, he played me a dog-rough sketch of this song.

Gradually it evolved into a parable of the conflict between the sacred and the profane, gospel and the blues, two musics that have often and wrongly been segregated. And B. B. King was a fitting choice since long before he'd migrated from Mississippi to Memphis, he'd began his musical career singing in a gospel quartet.

The duet also reverses the usual roles. Bono takes the early verses that are a parable of a blues singer whereas B. B. King has the final verse of redemption and gets to sing 'I was there when they crucified my Lord'. Of course, the question posed is that 'When Love Comes To Town', are gospel and the blues really polar and irreconcilable opposites?

## HEARTLAND

WITH 'Heartland', the album turns the corner. An orphan from *The Joshua Tree* recorded at Adam Clayton's home, it could be an impression of the Mississippi Delta seen from 10,000 feet up through a heat-haze and the windows of the Viscount aircraft they were using on this tour. The history-books and the golden oldies have been put aside; U2 are back dancing to their own drum.

## GOD PART II

A SIBLING of 'Hawkmoon 269', this starts with bare bass and drums that could have been on any Plastic Ono Band record. U2 are facing forward again and Bono's switching the apparent terms of the whole album, now complaining 'I don't believe in the Sixties in the golden age of pop/You glorify the past

when the future dries up'. Indeed the basic song can be heard as a precursor of *Achtung Baby*. The main difference is Jimmy Iovine's production style which puts Bono in the forefront of the mix.

Again love is the only spar to which Bono can cling. He's hurtling along the same helter-skelter as John Lennon, berating Albert Goldman for his blaspheming biography of the Beatle yet also confessing 'I don't believe that rock'n'roll can really change the world'.

'God Part II' takes all the contradictions head-on; Bono can only find relief in the line of the Canadian and radical Christian singer-songwriter, Bruce Cockburn, who says 'he's gonna kick the darkness till it bleeds daylight'.

## STAR SPANGLED BANNER/ BULLET THE BLUE SKY

THE LONE track from the final date of the 1987 tour, Tempe Arizona, December 20. The band had reinforced the Hendrix connection by prefacing all concert performances with a 43-second segment from his Woodstock performance of the US national anthem while Edge's own playing had developed into a deep cloud of foreboding, a far more tortured and extravagantly grim mood than even the studio original. This was in tune with his own development since initially he'd been the band member least convinced by Bono's American enthusiasms. But once converted, he gave his all as this performance confirms.

Bono's rap had also been extended. Now he was explaining what he really meant in the original line, 'a man breathes deep into a saxophone', as he spoke of being 'back in the hotel room with John Coltrane and *A Love Supreme*'. There was also the first sense of the media disorientation of *Achtung Baby* as he shouts 'I can't tell the difference between ABC news, *Hill Street Blues* and a preacher on the old time gospel hour, stealing money from the old and the sick.'

The transfiguring music of John Coltrane versus the spiritual frauds of the Moral Majority, the higher spirit of Jimi Hendrix at Woodstock, these were the sources of artistic liberation U2 were trying to expose to their new audience.

## ALL I WANT IS YOU

T HE FINAL track should have clued in the critics who accused U2 of revivalism. The basic design of the song would have suited *The Unforgettable Fire* but their experiences since take 'All I Want Is You' into another dimension.

The early playing is most restrained with only Van Dyke Parks' string arrangement hinting at how the track would blossom. All the frenzy and storms seem over and Bono's singing is calming and assured. The final pact of love is made and then suddenly in the last three minutes, the mood shifts once again. Bono repeatedly shouts 'I want to take you higher' while Edge surpasses even himself with one of his most perfectly logical and emotional passages as Van Dyke Parks' strings arise from the mix.

Then the band falls silent to let the strings play the last dizzy coda. A final, book-ending reference to The Beatles since *Rattle And Hum* could be seen as their 'A Year In The Life'? Or a hint that U2 were already moving on? In any book, 'All I Want Is You' is superb, mature pop.

# Achtung Baby

## U28; released October 1991

*A CHTUNG BABY* **CAUGHT EVERYONE BY SURPRISE. AND INTENTIONALLY SO.** Hurt by the mixed reception given *Rattle And Hum* in all its incarnations, U2 vanished into the long grass and plotted. And then once *Achtung Baby* appeared, U2 untypically became publicity shy, abstaining from interviews and preferring to let critics and the public make their own unaided assessment.

*Achtung Baby* or 'danger baby' – its title a quip by the band's veteran Cork soundman Joe O'Herlihy – was seen as U2 making their most audacious shift in style since *The Unforgettable Fire*. But they had left some earlier clues as to their direction. In 1990, they covered 'Night And Day' for the AIDS benefit album of Cole Porter songs, *Red Hot And Blue*. By recording in Berlin's Hansa Studios, they'd effectively signalled that the European side of their character now had the upper hand over the American and that they were abdicating as curators of any sacred rock'n'roll pantheon. Then Brian Eno, now re-established as their producer with Daniel Lanois, adroitly deputised in the promotional role, writing a keynote feature on the album for *Rolling Stone*.

One regularly requoted sequence defined the album for the media: 'Buzzwords on this record were trashy, throwaway, dark, sexy and industrial (all good) and earnest, polite, sweet, righteous, rockist and linear (all bad)'. Critics generally concurred, absolved U2 of past sins and approved *Achtung Baby* as an album of brave re-invention.

I have to confess that I didn't and still don't buy into that critical consensus. It demeaned and misunderstood *Rattle And Hum*, missed the continuities between the two albums and set up too stark a dividing line between the pair. *Achtung Baby* played games with their frame but they were already questioning it on *Rattle And Hum*. Nor had U2 ceased to write of spiritual matters. Bono might parade as 'The Fly' but 'Until The End Of The World' could be read as a dialogue between Jesus and Judas Iscariot (or even Mary Magdalene).

There were even musical links since 'Love Is Blindness' had been written during the *Rattle And Hum* sessions. Earlier tracks like both 'Hawkmoon 269' and 'God Part 2' are close relatives to the material on '*Achtung Baby*' while 'One' would be the rock ballad to make Axl Rose weep. And as the Zoo TV tour would confirm, Elvis Presley was still a source of wonder. The difference: he was now cast in his later role as the King of Las Vegas Trash, the man imitated in Sun City not the sanctified wonderworker of Sun Studios.

What did radically change was the production policy. On *Rattle And Hum*, Jimmy Iovine took a direct Route One approach but now they reverted to Lanois and Eno's oblique strategies with the sound far less compressed. If Bono's vocals had always been dramatically centre-stage, now he was a more elusive presence, playing with a new set of vocal characters, while Edge abstained from his previous bright, echoing trademark tones and Adam and Larry were given a more prominent role in the mix. And, of course, they had been affected by the prevailing cultural weather. U2 weren't to be silenced or made redundant by the new dance-rock styles emanating from the Madchester faction. Larry and especially Adam had the incentive to outplay their juniors, and the bassist, once charged with being their weakest musical member, is a powerful presence throughout.

They made the difference since Bono and Edge now knew they could confidently vary the band's focus and attach U2 to any shifts in pop fashion without the joins showing. U2's versatility stems from Mullen and Clayton's versatility and U2 would further court the dance audience by inviting Paul Oakenfield to remix 'Even Better Than The Real Thing', the conclusive evidence of their flexibility as masters of pop. The track also showed U2 weren't unhappy as hedonists. But then the band's friends and their most perceptive fans knew the image of them as stern-faced moralists had long been false. If nothing else, *Achtung Baby* freed U2 from the pressures of false expectations by readjusting the balance between their private selves and the often mistaken public perceptions of them.

Their choice of Berlin as a recording venue lent further symbolism. After the collapse of Communism, U2 were now back at the heart of a reuniting Europe. Berlin was the Continent's most profane place, the crossroads zoo city of Europe's darkest dreams. Furthermore its Hansa studio was the scene of Eno's previous triumphs with David Bowie. Many writers would follow the trail back to *Low*, using Edge's sparse, harsh and nettling guitar work as their signpost.

Indeed Bowie was almost the album's spiritual father-figure. Lypton Village was returning to its own teen glam roots when Bono had first been amazed by *Hunky Dory* and Gavin Friday had worn a dress. Bono's early singing had been littered with habits borrowed from Bowie and his role playing in the succeeding Zoo TV tour would probably have been unthinkable without Ziggy Stardust.

But then Bono had been making new acquaintances in the run-up to the album. Bowie was one but he'd become pally with Frank Sinatra too. 'So Cruel' and 'Love Is Blindness' also show a new cabaret influence; Jacques Brel and Scott Walker had entered the building.

In this, he'd been partially influenced by his soulmate Gavin Friday, who'd once run Dublin's Blue Jaysus club and was now signed to Island. 'Rock'n'Roll is a pussycat, dead and buried in the USA' he'd sung on 'Falling Off The Edge Of The World'. Both his solo Island albums are fascinating companion pieces to the new U2.

The notion of U2 recording in Hansa added to the mystery of the project but the reality is less romantic. The *Achtung Baby* may have been born in Berlin but it was fleshed out in later spring and summer sessions in Dublin. Again they set up house, this time at a seashore mansion, Elsinore, near Bono and Edge's homes, before final remixing involving both Flood and a returning Steve Lillywhite at Windmill.

Then there was the bootleg controversy. Tapes of the Hansa sessions surfaced in Germany and Holland but since they essentially comprised Bono wordlessly yodelling over fragments, they confirm how much later work was done at Elsinore. Some cynics suspected a scam, a pre-release ploy to boost interest but Dublin observers had another theory; they'd seen various U2 members casually leave tapes visible on the seats of their cars.

Achtung Baby may have rehabilitated U2's dented critical reputation, but after Zooropa it increasingly seems a transitional album for the band. In contradiction to the maxims of Eno's Rolling Stone manifesto, three of its most enduring tracks may turn out to be the ballads, 'One', 'So Cruel' and 'Love Is Blindness' while 'Who's Gonna Ride Your Wild Horses' isn't so much – to use Eno's terms – 'trashy' and 'throwaway' as one of the weakest and most obvious melodies the mature U2 had produced. There are definitely moments when you can feel U2 are summoning all their craft and studio experience to escape from tight corners.

The album was also curiously untimely. After all, U2 had spent the Eighties opposing the materialism of the decade, only to examine and flirt with those values on an album released in 1991. Again, they were responding to the confused backlash against Rattle And Hum. On its release that album seemed a mess of contradictions – how could four squillionaires preach against material corruption? – but Rattle And Hum is most powerful exactly because it is the spontaneous diary of a band on the run, freshly discovering and still surprised by those questions, without the time or the space for reflection or undue self-consciousness.

So on Achtung Baby U2 most deliberately stepped off the soap-box. Painful personal politics topped its agenda and, especially on 'So Cruel' and 'Love Is Blindness', Bono was recognising that his earlier ideals of religious and romantic self-surrender could no longer be expressed so simply.

But at points Achtung Baby can look over-calculated. U2 can seem to be trying too hard to be simple, second-guessing their critics as if they're trying to write to the approved script. They and obviously the Bono of 'The Fly' are most unsure about whether or not 'a conscience is a pest'.

One reason for this uncertainty could be their long time away from the stage without direction or nourishment from their audience. U2's best work has usually arisen when they have found an ideal balance between their instincts and their perfectionism but on Achtung Baby they can seem to be groping their way through a welter of conflicting advice and stimuli.

But, of course, Achtung Baby doesn't stand alone. The three-ring mixed media circus of the Zoo TV tour embellished the stronger material and rescued the weaker tracks of the album. Far more importantly, it refocused the band. Zooropa would be a far more coherent and creatively confident record.

---

## ZOO STATION

THIS TIME, U2 didn't start an album with any bridge-building tactics or concessions to their former music. Instead they cut the cables as Edge reverses in with a backwards grumble of feedback like a motor-cycle in suspended animation. A piano tinkles on tip-toes and

Larry's drums are industrialised as U2 set off on a strange new trip down the arteries of Berlin's train network.

It's a song of new anticipations and appetites. Bono's a new style of Fool, 'ready for the laughing gas... ready for what's next... ready to let go of the steering wheel' on an existential mission now he's realised that 'Time is a train/Makes the future past' and that he's two steps down the line from Berlin's Zoological Gardens, looking for the Phoenix in its park.

It's also a fizzy and carefree new brand of glam-rock, a sprightlier retracing of David Bowie's path on *Low* in its mixture of Spartan rhythms and sudden flurries of melody. This is U2's invite to their own Magical Mystery Menagerie.

## EVEN BETTER THAN THE REAL THING

ONE SONG, two versions of an idea that had been around since the 'Rattle And Hum' sessions. In its first (album) incarnation, 'Even Better...' tipped another glam-rock wink to Marc Bolan and then the second (single) version, with Paul Oakenfield's total restructuring, found U2 cheekily ascending into rave heaven. Rock bands with almost 15 years on the career clock weren't supposed to take up this sort of challenge and then demolish the competition. But then they key to the refashioning of this cunningly arranged song was the chorus. Singing 'take me higher', U2

could still steal some American soul and gospel tricks for their Europop.

It's also the first real clue to the Zoo TV expedition and its mission to rearrange clichés like the antique Coca-Cola slogan. Virtual reality isn't virtuous and appearances are enjoyed exactly because they might be deceptive as Bono pleads to 'slide down the surface of things'. He didn't want to teach the world to sing either. There might be irony but the music, especially in the Oakenfield remix, is so exhilarating, it's beyond bothering about such scruples. U2 had digested the disco lesson 'on the dance floor, everyone is a performer'.

## ONE

U2 MIGHT have been shape-shifting on *Achtung Baby* but 'One' was the album's insurance policy, the rock ballad to beguile American radio programmers. But if its basic ingredients were pretty standard, its secret was the sauce. Whereas other bands would have fallen into temptation and plastered 'One' with a barrage of guitars and keyboards, U2 let the song breathe and didn't drown Larry and Adam in the final mix.

But there's both continuity and development. The playing is patterned like the U2 of their own Sun Studio sessions but warped by Lanois, Eno and Flood's mix. Just like 'I Still Haven't Found What I'm Looking For', the stresses don't quite fall where they should. The rhythms are more horse and buggy than

Euro autopilot before Edge's guitar finally flares at the end. The result: a creation that partakes in equal measure from both Europe and America.

Still, by the band's own account, 'One' was a lifesaver since it was born at a critical juncture in the album's creation. In the early Berlin sessions, they were getting frustrated, still casting around for a new direction and inspiration. But Edge found the key to the safe when he delivered the basic melody for 'One'.

Come the time of Zoo TV, the song would be adopted as a pro-gay, anti-AIDS anthem since a section of the accompanying video was directed by a dying victim of the disease, David Wojnarowcz. Certainly there were allusions that could fit that interpretation but, truth to tell, 'One' was universal, speaking to any two partners, roped into the mutual bondage of an abusive and fractious relationship.

## UNTIL THE END OF THE WORLD

EDGE'S marriage had broken down so many spotted references to its collapse in lines like 'we were so close together as bride and groom'. Again, it was a misleading interpretation. Instead, officially, the song explores the relationship between Judas Iscariot and Jesus. It even broaches the possibility of Judas' ultimate redemption.

Bono takes the part of Judas yet that isn't its only weird element. Judas is the bride to Christ's groom

and then describes the kiss of betrayal in Gethsemane as 'in the garden I was playing the tart'. Judas and Christ in a gay relationship? Or is there another layer, conscious or otherwise in the lyric? Replace Judas with Mary Magdalene and you could have an archetypal song about the clash between carnal and spiritual love.

## WHO'S GONNA RIDE YOUR WILD HORSES

THIS ONE doesn't work. A very ordinary tune, a lot of flailing riffing, a murky mix as camouflage and the sense that it's possibly stitched together from two earlier and entirely separate compositions. The sleeve credits note that it was produced by Lanois, Eno and Steve Lillywhite. Hmmm... this sounds like song surgeons at work. The single version of this song, as remixed with Paul Barrett in Dublin, replaces Edge's guitars with keyboards with a more satisfactory result.

## SO CRUEL

BONO cited Scott Walker as an influence here but this ballad of romantic masochism may also owe some slight debt to Roy Orbison with whom he and Edge had collaborated on the Big O's final comeback hit, 'Mystery Girl'. That successful production had confirmed the pair's graduation as popmeisters and 'So Cruel', founded on piano patterns, builds its passion through stealth and suspense.

No games, this is finally the real Real Thing. Romantic love curdles into a scary possessiveness and claustrophobic jealousy yet there's an eerie sweetness in the pain and sorrow, as if torment and rapture are kissing cousins. We could be back at 'With Or Without You' but now we're listening to the song's aftermath with both its protagonists weighed down by all the burdens of their experiences since. Bryan Ferry might have been the first to claim 'Love Is A Drug' but 'So Cruel' spoke of such an addiction that the dosage must always be increased. Or that little death is only the first murder of a lover's self-esteem.

## THE FLY

BONO described this as 'the sound of four men chopping down *The Joshua Tree*' in an early communication with the band's own official fanzine *Propaganda*, and 'The Fly' was deliberately released as the album's first single to reinforce that point and prepare the audience for its new sound.

U2 might have celebrated the 'Angel Of Harlem' on the preceding album but they'd kept within the safe confines of traditional R&B. But if they'd previously preferred to avoid the Rap revolution, 'The Fly' was their own belated acknowledgement of the transformation.

What was spectacular about *Achtung Baby* was that no other band in the universe could switch through contrasting styles as 'So Cruel' and 'The Fly'. Edge takes charge of this collage almost as if he's sampling himself, Adam Clayton and Larry Mullen see off all pretenders to their throne, and what separates this track from the Madchester scene is its refusal to be intimidated by the most brutal Black Music sound of the Eighties. If much British rock/dance music set itself up as an alternative to Hip Hop, U2 weren't joining that exclusion zone.

Meanwhile Bono played against type, having finally digested the lesson that charlatans and gurus often inhabit the same body. Again like Bowie, he was showing a new talent for vocal mimicry, confidently rapping and soaring off into his Fat Lady falsetto.

## MYSTERIOUS WAYS

AGAIN U2 invade the dance floor but more conventionally. Edge erupts with a taut and thunderous intro and Adam's reggae lessons finally pay off. Of course, what struck many commentators on its release was Bono's couplet 'If you want to kiss the sky/Better learn how to kneel' with its reference to cunnilingus but then, maybe, he knew about sheela-na-gigs in Irish chapels long before P.J. Harvey. Besides, the position was consistent with an album that was so saturated with the theme of obsessive sexual adoration.

## TRYIN' TO THROW YOUR ARMS AROUND THE WORLD

WELL GLAZED and marinaded, Bono's stumbling around the pavements at dawn bound for the early houses. And though it's dedicated to LA's celebrity shebeen, The Flaming Colossus, the walking or, rather, the swaying pace of the music doesn't so much suit California stretch limo culture as someone on the Dublin circuit between Lillie's Bordello, Suesey Street, and the final egg, chips and black coffee pit-stop at the Manhattan.

Some of this album's throwaways don't always convince but this is endearing in its pronounced sense of the ridiculous, though the line about 'a fish needs a bicycle' was positively antique, a graffiti washed off the walls of most Dublin loos before U2 were even formed. Meanwhile the band chuckle and whistle on the sidelines and Brian Eno's keyboards catch the birdsong in the Dublin dawn as Bono renews the pledge to be home soon.

## ULTRA VIOLET (LIGHT MY WAY)

U2 MIGHT claim to re-inventing themselves but this track reverts to their earliest musical principles. Edge's tone might be darker, like an update of the Motown telegraph key guitar sound, but this cut is an echo of U2's original repeato-riff formula.

Again Bono's bewildered by a relationship under strain, uneasy with obligations, uncomfortable finding solace in another's charity but the band don't sufficiently develop the initial idea to warrant the five minutes of 'Ultra Violet'.

## ACROBAT

'DON'T LET the bastards grind you down'. Another love song or U2's riposte to their critics? Again Bono's refusing to be enlisted in any religious or political club, testifying 'I'd break bread and wine/If there was a church I could receive in', comparing himself to an acrobat but, for the third time on the album, the lyric is let down by some rather ordinary riffing.

## LOVE IS BLINDNESS

THE COMPANION to 'So Cruel', U2 introduce the blues to the cabaret and leave both emotionally devastated. Yet again, love is both a nightmare and a necessity, an experience that can only be navigated with the utmost humility.

But this performance is beyond any poetics on Bono's part. It's far beyond rock as it's normally known, given most acts' abject failure – besides Bryan Ferry in his prime – whenever they were tempted to enter the world of Jacques Brel. It's certainly far, far more than pastiche with Edge's guitar lines, part mournful melody, part odd, stabbed blues interjections, essential to the song's mood of exhausted emotional disorientation.

# Zooropa

U29; released July 1993

**I**F *ACHTUNG BABY* **SOMETIMES SHOWS SIGNS OF STRESS,** *ZOOROPA* **WAS A FAR** more creatively relaxed album. The Zoo TV tour may have been obsessed with media overload and all its static but *Zooropa* flows naturally and elegantly as if all four members were never off the same wavelength during its making. Surely, U2 never made an album of such composure.

Bono called it 'a surreal pop album' and his description fits. Except for the opening title track, Edge abstains from guitar assault tactics, preferring to underplay or seek new textures from his various keyboard paint-boxes. Bono's singing is intimate and he never sounds as if he's addressing a meeting. Adam and Larry's contribution are founded on selection and simplicity. The tight schedule for recording the album may also have meant they were never tempted into over-fussy perfectionism.

*Zooropa* also finds a distance U2 didn't always establish on *Achtung Baby*. Tracks like 'Numb' and 'Some Days Are Better Than Others' are droll and poker-faced; Bono's often content to be a comparatively non-committal observer as on 'Daddy's Gonna Pay For Your Crashed Car', and the final distracting device is their recruitment of Johnny Cash for 'The Wanderer'. On *Zooropa* U2 cast themselves more as producers and directors than actors and they wear it well.

As with *Rattle And Hum*, U2 had used touring for stimulus. Initially conceived as a mini-album, *Zooropa* just grew and grew and was recorded during a break from touring through spring 1993 in three Dublin studios: The Factory, Westland and the new Windmill Lane facilities which had moved after the original Windmill set-up had closed down. The production credits also changed; Daniel Lanois was promoting his own solo album, so Flood became Eno's partner with Edge assisting.

This was how albums used to be produced in the Sixties and Seventies when acts didn't wander cold into the studio. Working off the momentum of Zoo TV, the U2 quartet had obviously rebonded and don't sound as if they're renewing each other's acquaintance. The off-stage experiments weren't distractions but used as the source of new material as the band explored the technological menagerie of Zoo TV.

But the tour's themes and celebrity cast had changed since the late Eighties. Out went Bob Dylan and Sun Studios in Memphis; in came the Cyberpunk agenda of William Gibson and supermodels Naomi Campbell and Christy Turlington. Once U2 had prided themselves on their authenticity; now, they found their own strange loops in the artificial. Any last streak of Puritanism had been erased.

Compassion also replaces judgement. In the universe of *Zooropa*, everyone's electronically linked into a network of voyeurism. The television viewer, watching 'Babyface' flaunting herself on late-night cable, is in no position to criticise her. Bono describes rather than prescribes.

He's definitely more comfortable as U2's Irish celebrity correspondent. His conscience isn't silent but neither is it a nagging pest. God-bothering has been replaced by a fascination with celebrity as some sort of hologram, the new symbol for the angels and devils in his head. And if U2's music once seemed as if it aimed to scorch the daylight sky, now it bleeps and cruises like some enigmatic Satellite of Love, primarily for nocturnal viewing only.

The success of *Achtung Baby* and Zoo TV simultaneously relaxed and kick-started them. They never sound as if they have to invade some other act's turf and prove themselves to a younger audience as the next Nirvana or whatever. On *Zooropa*, U2 take only what they need and no more.

And yet like so much of U2's work, *Zooropa* follows a deceptive path. The final track, 'The Wanderer', turns the tables again. With guest vocals from Johnny Cash, U2 suddenly escape the penthouse and return to the pavements, away from the champagne set and back on the Thunderbird wine. Only this time U2 may have learned from Sergio Leone and Wim Wenders that it's wiser for Europeans to treat America as dreamtime not reality. 'The Wanderer' is intelligently both authentic and artificial, the scriptures rewritten for a spaghetti Western, the gospels according to the disciple, Clint. Imagine an Elvis Presley version recorded in Las Vegas; it may be the best clue as to their next destination.

---

## ZOOROPA

AMERICANS have truckers but the EU has no pop culture myths, just the ghost of Kraftwerk on the Trans-European Express. So the title track is suitably vague and other-worldly: the music, the whispered babble of satellite components with no analogy to the chatter of MTV Europe's presenters.

So *Zooropa* exists where night-time radio channels merge to talk in competing tongues and only the adverts for the most familiar brand-names supply any common litany and language. All Bono can do is open the song by invoking the 'Vorsprung durch Technik' slogan, confess he has 'no compasses' and 'no map' and hope his audience will understand his notion that rock's role is to 'dream out loud'.

Earlier U2 patchwork quilts didn't always work musically but not here. Shrouded behind the opening piano part, voices hum like cybernetic crickets before Edge enters with a guitar melody whose sweep is more sombre than sweet. Then, after almost four minutes of overture, the band dig in with a new and more hopefully urgent groove, captured by Joe O'Herlihy at a soundcheck. U2 may be lost in the ozone but unblinkingly so. As Bono says: 'Uncertainty can be a guiding light' and only imagination can be a compass.

## BABYFACE

THE FIRST of the album's restrained miniatures. Again Bono's lyric is multi-layered. It can be superficially read as a love song except that this affair is also an interface with satellite porn with the question of its last line – 'How could beauty be so kind to an ordinary guy?' – entering a tender trap far beyond the usual uses of irony.

Meanwhile a glockenspiel tinkles, Larry lazily slaps a snare and U2 keep the music controlled at minimalist demo levels, only flaring in the vocal harmonies of the chorus, an appropriate strategy since this song could be U2's sweet companion to Lou Reed's 'Satellite Of Love'. The song is sweet but its characters are connected only by transductors. This is ourselves as the new alien life-force.

## NUMB

AS ESCAPEE from the Berlin *Achtung Baby* sessions, later reworked. With its basic loop taken from a passage in Leni Reifenstahl's *Triumph Of The Will*, her Nazi propaganda film of the 1934 Nuremberg Rally, 'Numb' is Edge confirming the basic rules of mutant rap that it can be anything you want to imagine as long as it conforms to the basic

principles of matching the spoken word with suitable beats. Since the loop came from an obedient drummer aged 11, 'Numb' can be interpreted as a satire on totalitarianism but again, the listener can choose other angles. Like Edge playing Buster Keaton in one of Samuel Beckett's black comedies, effectively rewriting the dramatist's basic premise:'I can't go on, I must go on.'

It *is* desperately funny, the ultimate confession of the jaded rock star taken to the most ridiculous proportions over assembly-line rhythms roboticised with the Kraftwerk touch while Edge adds a cheesy, meandering keyboard fill on 'arcade sounds'. But just to ensure 'Numb' isn't unrelentingly grim, Bono adds a subtext in his Fat Lady falsetto, still yearning 'gimme some more of that stuff love'. Larry's harmonies are also buried somewhere in the mix.

## LEMON

FROM ONE angle, 'Lemon' is the album's most familiar and conventional track, leaving the listener wondering where exactly are the separations of the Talking Heads of *Remain In Light*, Brian Eno and U2. The similarities are further underlined by Eno's contributions on synths, strings and backing vocals while Bono's lyrics – 'A man makes a picture... a man captures colour' – use one of David Byrne's most characteristic distancing effects.

But they pastiche it well, the song cruising and wafting along with such assurance exactly because Larry and Adam have no trouble emulating the dream team of Chris Frantz and Tina Weymouth. As for Bono, she who's 'Lemon' in the title is enshrined as 'imagination'. Somewhere along the line in the making of *Achtung Baby* and *Zooropa*, the Goddess had entered the building.

## STAY (FARAWAY SO CLOSE)

ALSO reincarnated on the Wim Wenders movie of the same name, 'Stay...' is another cubist song, drifting in and out of its many dreamscapes. Bono's protagonist could be a poor little career celebrity rich girl on the nightclub shift anywhere between Dublin and Los Angeles, 'dressed up like a car crash' mechanically stopping for cigarettes at a Seven-Eleven even though she doesn't smoke. Yet she's also 'a vampire or a victim' and even more distractingly another multimedia angel, 'faraway, so close', like the Almighty, ubiquitous on global satellite distribution.

Intimacy dissolves, waxes and wanes, conflicting appearances get bewildering and again like 'Babyface', the drums are slack and lazy and the melody on its knees in puzzled adoration. This chorus is meant to soar yet it can't fend off Bono's uneasiness so the dream ends, collapsing and waking up in a hotel room to Larry Mullen's final matter-of-fact downbeat. As so often on *Zooropa*, sound and sentiment rarely ride in easy tandem.

## DADDY'S GONNA PAY FOR YOUR CRASHED CAR

'AN INDUSTRIAL blues', according to Bono in a preview interview with Joe Jackson of *Hot Press*. But what industrial blues begins with a blast of Stalinist realist ceremonial muzak, 'A Fanfare' from the album Lenin's *Favourite Songs* on the Soviet label Melodia?

Still, once U2 bolt in the foundation loop, Edge, Adam and Larry cram in their contributions 'til no more can be processed or compressed into this black hole of sound. Another female nightclub feature but this time, Bono's far from seduced by this 'precious stone'. She has no hidden depths; his lyric needs none either.

## SOME DAYS ARE BETTER THAN OTHERS

AROUND about here, *Zooropa* moves out of celebrity lane. Or at least rents a room on the Hangover Hotel where 'some days the bouncers won't let you in' on a song that revolves around Adam's liquid bass line. Yet again, U2 are being economical with their sonic truth.

The angels have been escorted off the premises and Bono's just alone in his perfectionist head. Edge slants in with a guitar passage of jerky irritation and for the first time on *Zooropa*, Bono's fallen back to Earth, 'lookin' for Jesus and his mother'.

## THE FIRST TIME

BY ITS ARRANGEMENT, you mightn't realise that this song was originally written with Al Green in mind. The music is closer to the pallor of The Velvet Underground at their most treacherously quiet, 'Heroin' before its rush to misjudgement, but the sentiments are true to the evolution of *Zooropa* as U2 redirect their search for salvation.

Bono claimed the song followed the path of the Prodigal Son, an apt theme for Al Green who returned from soul stardom to the preacher's podium not long after a girlfriend exacted revenge by scalding him with piping hot grits. A song whose grace is in its nakedness, U2 again show how they'd gained from their new musical slimline diet before Bono gets to deliver a few bluesy Brooce-like hollers as it fades over the horizon.

## DIRTY DAY

A MURKY, broody intro with sinister bubbling keyboards precede this tale of gloom. Bono's not usually one to sink into brooding despair but this time the Fat Lady's ill-temperedly singing 'Throw a rock in the air/You're bound to hit someone guilty'. A song about emotional torpor and poison, the guitars re-enter to give him a dressing-down before he quite with the line, 'The days run away like horses over the hills'. We're definitely far removed from *Zooropa* now.

## THE WANDERER

THROUGH the previous three tracks, the world of *Zooropa* has been imploding and now Johnny Cash walks in. As with 'The First Time', this wasn't intended for their own use but for Cash's own recording but 'The Wanderer' became the perfect subversive epilogue to the album.

Bono thought this was U2 as the Holiday Inn From Hell Band and it really was country'n'Kraftwerk, Ennio Morricone in Nashville as remixed by Yello, a jolt to anyone still sufficiently foolish and purist to believe rock fame involves the recycling of any single style.

The quest continued; only the scenery changed. Bono's lyrics are back in the Bible Belt but then it too was another land of late-night television temptation with its preacher just a remote control touch and one channel away from 'Babyface'.

Even so, 'The Wanderer' concerned far more than post-modernist media comparisons. It was intentionally Biblical, a parable of a lone just man searching for truth. You can have fun imagining Elvis Presley singing this but Johnny Cash, the only convincing American icon left, was the ideal interpreter. And yet it's far from humourless. This is the seeker who 'went out for the papers/Told her I'd be home by noon'. Could the wanderer be another Prodigal Son?

Think about it. Listening back

over U2's output, you can detect uncanny and constant links between their present and earliest past. 'The Wanderer' is cut from the same cloth as their first ever album track 'I Will Follow'. What's that chorus that goes 'Walkaway, walkaway, walkaway'?

---

# Passengers: Original Soundtracks 1

Island CID 8043; released November 1995

**W**HAT WOULD U2 SOUND LIKE IF THEY WEREN'T TOO BUSY BEING U2? Pick up a copy of *Passengers: Original Soundtracks 1* to find out. A mostly instrumental record, it was recorded over a two week session in London's Westside studio in November 1994 and another five weeks in Dublin in the summer of 1995.

"It used to be said that a lot of English rock'n'roll bands went to art school. We went to Brian," Bono told *The Daily Telegraph*'s Neil McCormick, "Brian has been part of our set-up for the past 10 years. We just wanted to make a record where he was in charge. It won't be for everybody, but it's a real trip. Sort of late-night-in-a-fast-car music. We were just happy to be in his backing band."

To find out how this album came together we have to go back to the *Zooropa* sessions. Work had gone relatively smoothly, but as the record neared completion, the band – as Eno remembers, hit "a stone wall". To break the stalemate, he suggested the band do some improvising sessions, hoping that just playing and not bothering with the finer details of recording would clear the heads. The sessions proved to be so productive, U2 and Eno returned to the studio after the ZOO TV tour in the summer of 1994. There they were joined by Howie B. Howie had first met U2 when he worked on Bono's version of Leonard Cohen's song 'Hallelujah' which appeared on the Cohen tribute CD *Tower of Song*.

They imagined they would make 'film music' and then find a film for it later. Up to 25 hours of improvisation were recorded, from which the *Original Soundtracks 1* album was distilled. It took only two months to make, mostly because Eno spent a great deal of time on preproduction. He set the mood in the studio by decorating it with sundry objects and fabrics from Africa, India and the Middle East as well as bringing in a wealth of sequences and rhythm tracks. He set up a large screen and a stack of videos for inspiration such as news footage from the Fifties, animations from students at the Royal College of Art, and Japanese animé films. Anything to break out of a rut and lots of different textures to suit any situation. Eno also suggested band members switch instruments. It gave them the opportunity to express a side that their studio albums had no room for.

With Eno as bandleader and U2 his 'session musicians' the hybrid result turned out more interesting than sceptics feared. *Original Soundtracks 1* captures U2 at their most laid back. U2 are seen taking baby steps into the ambient-meets-pop world otherwise occupied by the likes of David Sylvian. Not that this was completely new territory for the band's guitar player. The Edge after all had worked with Jah Wobble and Holger Czukay on the François Kevorkian produced instrumental LP *Snake Charmer* (1983).

The *Passengers* project spawned an unexpected hit single with 'Miss Sarajevo'. Even Larry Mullen – who has publicly stated his dislike of the *Passengers* album – could find no fault with it. It later made it to U2's second *Best Of* compilation.

The extensive sleeve notes (signed by Ben O'Rian and C.S.J. Bofop – an anagram and a letter-shift version of b.r.i.a.n. e.n.o.) are mostly fictional. They'd be pretentious if they weren't taking the piss so much and weren't riddled with in-jokes, anagrams and other word games. Consider the character Eno comes up with: 'Peter von Heineken' (Paul McGuiness), 'Venda Davis' (Dave Evans), Tanya McLoad (Adam Clayton), Kiley Sue LaLonne (Anne-Louise Kelly, the album production manager) and Pi Hoo Sun, none other than P. Hewson (Bono's real name). Only three of the films Eno describes on the album sleeve are real: *Miss Sarajevo, Ghost In The Shell,* and *Beyond The Clouds*.

Originally, the band had pictured a collection of tunes with a late-night feel, in the vein of *Achtung Baby*'s 'Love is Blindness'. They were thinking of calling the album *The Blue Record*. But things changed along the way. Travel became a *leit motif* for the band on this project. (Six years before they made the heart-in-a-suitcase an icon on the Elevation tour!). On a black board in the studio someone wrote: 'Make the music of the future you want to live in.'

As that music turned out a little more experimental than they'd expected, in the end the band chickened out of releasing what they had created under their own name, afraid of committing commercial suicide. The travelling idea had stuck so *Passengers* became the name of the group. Beside U2 and Eno the loose collective included maestro Luciano Pavarotti, DJ Howie B, Japanese singer Holi as well as Island Records art director Cally. (The picture he used on the sleeve of the album was taken from a Czechoslovakian book from the sixties about the future of space travel.)

*Original Soundtracks 1* isn't an easy ride. If you like your music in straightforward chunks and prefer the U2 of 'Sunday Bloody Sunday' and

'Out Of Control', this album's ambient meandering may not be for you. For those who dare, it offers a different perspective on the band you thought you knew. We get to see the world through their eyes and it's a fascinating angle. It's a view from the tops of Tokyo buildings, life seen through a lens, peeking through peep holes, looking down on earth from outer space. This ability to observe is essential to any artist's work. Like Iggy's journey man from 'Lust For Life': '... he sees things from under glass, he looks through his window's eye, he sees the things he knows are his, he sees the bright and hollow sky, he sees the city asleep at night, he sees the stars are out tonight.' It is the band's ability to see things differently that makes them the unique unit they are. And whatever they may call themselves, we know they're still U2.

---

## UNITED COLOURS OF PLUTONIUM

ZOO TV's last shows were played in Japan in December 1993. Not a good place to end a tour, Larry Mullen told *Q* Magazine: 'You can begin a tour in Japan, you can have the middle of a tour in Japan, but don't end a tour in Japan. It was, like, I am going mad...' The impact of these final days of the ZOO TV tour can be felt throughout *Original Soundtracks 1*.

Its title a pun on clothing manufacturer Benetton's slogan, 'United Colours Of Plutonium' tries to capture the sense of speed of Shinkansen, the bullet train that travels at an average of 164mph through the surreal neon world of downtown Tokyo.

## SLUG

ORIGINALLY entitled 'Seibu', after one of the top department store chains in Japan, 'Slug' sets the twinkle of Christmas decorations

against the thoughts of a desolate soul: 'Don't want what I deserve, don't want to change the frame, don't want to be a pain, don't wanna stay the same...'

## YOUR BLUE ROOM

'MISS SARAJEVO' was the single, but 'Your Blue Room' is probably the album's fan favourite. It features a rare vocal performance by Adam Clayton, whose elegantly spoken coda ends – as Bono calls it – this 'erotic hymn'. His words suggest a (blue) movie: 'Zooming in, zooming out, nothing I can't do without, a lens to see it all up close.' Like 'Do You Feel Loved' on *Pop*, the song considers the carnal tangle of a conversation, the secular and the sacred. Originally intended to be the second single, it was never released. A sought after 1996 promo of a radio edit with a fetching sleeve exists.

## ALWAYS FOREVER NOW

ENO OBLIQUELY heaps praise on The Edge in the sleeve notes for this piece, an anxious affirmation of life: 'The star role falls to Venda Davis, whose Zenlike rationality and pronounced muscularity form the psycho-physical axis around which the movie is constructed. The title's said to be based on a Damien Hirst picture. Hirst did publish a book called 'I Want to Spend the Rest of My Life Everywhere, with Everyone, One to One, Always, Forever, Now' in 1997. The song later re-appeared on the soundtrack for Michael Mann's film *Heat*, a Pacino, De Niro, Kilmer vehicle, alongside Eno's 'Force Maker.'

## A DIFFERENT KIND OF BLUE

THIS QUIET drone is narrated by Brian Eno. Stepping out of the blue room he offers a view from the higher ground: 'Those cars. All new. So small. Down there. From here. So high. We drift. We fly. With twilight breakthrough. A different kind of blue.' It's the shortest track on the album, based on a title and the beginnings of a Bono jazz song.

## BEACH SEQUENCE

FEATURING Bono on one-finger piano, 'Beach Sequence' – like 'Your Blue Room' before it – is linked to *Beyond The Clouds* in the sleeve notes. This is a real film by Michelangelo Antonioni and Wim Wenders. Antonioni had been crippled by a stroke and could not speak – his friends created the opportunity for him to direct a final film. *Beyond The Clouds* is about a direc-

tor who conjures up stories by simple observation. The four stories in the film explore how visual imagination defines love. Is this the '... new frame, a new perspective' and the '... lens to see it all up close' mentioned in 'Your Blue Room'?

## MISS SARAJEVO

THE ONLY single off the album is based on American journalist Bill Carter's documentary *Miss Sarajevo* which was produced and funded by Bono. The documentary captured life during wartime in Bosnia and focused on a surreal beauty pageant – organised by Sarajevans, defiantly getting on with their lives.

It was Pavarotti who initiated the collaboration. For weeks he placed increasingly insistent phone calls to Bono's house to try and get him to participate in the Pavarotti & Friends concert in Modena (September 12, 1995). Bono was too busy to answer. Exasperated, Pavarotti told the Hewsons' staff: "Tell 'God' to give me a call." Eventually, contact was made. Though pressed for time, Bono, The Edge and Brian Eno agreed to perform. But they asked the tenor for a favour in return. U2 convinced Pavarotti to sing their new song with them live in Modena and to record it in the studio for the album.

Pavarotti's lyrics, written to reflect the plight of the resilient Sarajevans and their unanswered call of help from the west, were translated for him by a friend of the band: "It's said that a river finds the way to the sea, and like the river you shall come to me, beyond the borders and the thirsty lands, you say that as a river, like a river... love shall come, love... and I'm not able to pray anymore, and I cannot hope for love anymore, and I cannot wait for love anymore..."

The single was released in aid of the War Child charity, and reached number 6 in the UK charts.

## ITO OKASHI

AKIKO KOBAYASHI had already built up a singer/songwriter career in Japan, when she decided to move to England and change her name to Holi. Her first English-language album *Under The Monkey Puzzle Tree* was produced by Steve Jansen and Mick Karn — both, like David Sylvian, ex-members of the band Japan. Brian Eno invited Holi to the studio, not telling her she would be working with U2. The Japanese lyrics were improvised by her on the day. "Let's talk about something beautiful," she sings, "On the face of this earth, something very close to you, about something that is tasteful, like something that makes the heart beat faster, certainly something is very pleasant..."

## ONE MINUTE WARNING

WHILE they were recording Passengers the band were commissioned to do a bit of score for the animated feature *Ghost In The Shell* by Mamoru Oshia. 'One Minute Warning' seemed to fit the request. The Edge's guitar is reminiscent of the intro of 'The Unforgettable Fire' (the song). Triggered by footage of Godard's *Alphaville*, buildings are said to be the inspiration behind 'One Minute Warning', but the lyrics speak of a 'lonesome soul, in an old black coat, a lonesome road' – which may or may not refer to *Ghost In The Shell*'s virtual protagonist, the 'ultimate secret agent of the future' who travels the information highways, but whose ultimate objective is to become truly human and exist outside of the net.

## CORPSE (THESE CHAINS ARE WAY TOO LONG)

THE EDGE doesn't get too many opportunities to showcase his voice. Only 'Seconds', 'Van Diemen's Land' and 'Numb' precede 'Corpse'. Listening to The Edge's plaintive vocal and the industrial noises in the background, one can but smile at the fact that twenty years into their career, U2 finally manage to sound like their old friends Virgin Prunes. 'Corpse' starts out with the crackle of a vinyl record and conjures up the monotony of life on the chain gang. It's a slow and sad modern blues. The Edge wanted to reflect on the limitations of the freedom that comes with success and money. Shackles can be a good thing for an artist to wear.

## ELVIS ATE AMERICA

WHILE Bono's previous song about the King, 'Elvis Presley And America' (from *The Unforgettable Fire*) was written on the microphone, 'Elvis Ate America' was put on paper before it was sung. Which is one of the reasons it's clever, witty and articulate where the older song was heartfelt but vague. Bono had written a poem, 'American David', for an art book printed in conjunction with the exhibition Elvis + Marilyn: 2 X Immortal: "Elvis loved America, God, the Bible, firearms, the movies, the office of presidency, junk food, drugs, cars, family, television, jewellery, straight talkin', dirty talkin' game shows, uniforms, and self-help books..." While the first two-thirds of the poem has little rhythm to it, the third part worked well as a lyric. With Howie B providing backing vocals, the blues rap took flight.

## PLOT 180

IT'S HARD to discern U2 in this track, a repetitive theme that is one of the album's truly cinematic pieces. The imaginary film title, *Hypnotize (Love me 'til Dawn)*, seems fitting and the accompanying sleeve notes amusingly cast 'Tony Corbin' (Anton Corbijn) as a chauffeur for a 'vindictive tabloid journalist', 'Pila Morgan' – whose name we cannot unscramble – though we suspect Eno means Piers Morgan, editor of Britain's Daily Mirror. Morgan caused outrage in 1995 with his headline Achtung Surrender! the day before an England v Germany football match.

## THEME FROM THE SWAN

NEAR THE end of the record, U2 seem to have dissolved in one of Eno's generative music pieces. The Edge has admitted to *Hot Press*'s Niall Stokes that this tune is 'mostly Brian'.

## THEME FROM LET'S GO NATIVE

THE BAND are back for a thumping finale. It's a bass driven jungle rumble that flirts with the Eno and David Byrne's collaboration *My Life In The Bush Of Ghosts*, but is a lot less angular. Even if this is Eno looping one of U2's improvisations, 'Theme From Let's Go Native' sounds like something the band could have played live and is reminiscent of their B-side 'The Three Sunrises'.

# Pop

Island CID U210, released March 97

**I**F **ACHTUNG BABY WAS THE SOUND OF FOUR MEN CHOPPING DOWN**
*The Joshua Tree*, *Pop* is the noise they made schlepping the giant cactus
home. Widely and wrongly regarded as the black sheep in U2's recording
history, *Pop* never really got the chance it deserved. It suffered from bad
press before it was ever released. Its late arrival hurt the subsequent tour as
the band went on the road, and they went on the road thinking the album
wasn't up to their standards. It was a vicious circle caused by bad planning,
not by bad songs.

But let's start with the beginning. What do you do when you come
down from the success that was *Achtung Baby* and the tours that
followed? You go back home, try to pick up your life, try to fix whatever was
broken after months of hard toil on the road. The Edge and Bono stayed in
Dublin. Adam and Larry went to New York to study music, believe it or not.

When it was time to embark on another recording journey, U2, Flood,
Howie B and Nellee Hooper got together with only half the rhythm section
present. Larry was recovering from spinal surgery. Nellee Hooper, a funk and
hip-hop aficionado, was a member of Bristol's Wild Bunch sound system
from which Massive Attack emerged. Hooper later went on to produce Soul
II Soul and was most sought after as a remixer.

Initially, the sessions were interesting. Flood, Howie and Nellee were
comfortable working with samples and loops. But at the end of the day the
material lacked 'soul'. It wasn't the technology. Flood put his finger on the
problem – it was the band who were sounding flat. The pressure was high,
as the PopMart tour had already been booked. Things didn't work out with
Hooper, but Howie B stayed on.

In his published diary, *A Year With Swollen Appendices*, Brian Eno says it
was Howie's "weird sense of space, his ability to leave things alone and let
the listener do the work" that gave him a job in U2's studio. The 'vibemaster'
himself saw his role as an aggravator, someone to challenge the band and
turn them on. He would lay down beats and introduce the band to music
they didn't know.

The team went to Miami where they spent two weeks in the studio.
Adam told the press they were working on a "rock-oriented album, heavy on
guitars". And that was the last time *Pop* was referred to as a rock album in
the press. The names Hooper, Howie B, and the references coming from the
band's camp (trip hop, techno, drum and bass, acid jazz), baffled a large part
of their audience. Then the media started reporting U2 were making a
'dance' album. Many fans were horrified before the album was even

released. Fans and critics alike forgot the band had flirted with dance music on *Achtung Baby*, getting Paul Oakenfold to remix 'Even Better Than The Real Thing'. They had sought the help of French DJ Francois Kevorkian to remix 'Two Hearts Beat As One' as far back as 1983.

When *Pop* was finally released, it was way past the original deadline. U2 had run out of time in the studio and were forced to hand in the album incomplete. "It's stuff that a lot of people probably wouldn't appreciate," The Edge later told Q magazine, "but it's a huge thing to let something go that you know you're not one-hundred percent with."

*Pop* suffered from multi-personality disorder. A 'dance album' that went by the name of *Pop*? As the kids say: way to confuse your audience! Bono later said a journalist had misquoted him. It was a 'dense' record, not a 'dance' record. Whether that's true or whether he was just being clever, we'll never know.

*Pop* is not a dance record. It is packed with guitar rock on top of an undercurrent of heavy, funky rhythms. It contains some extraordinary songs that deserve to be heard. 'Please' for example, 'Mofo' and 'Gone' – two key songs to the puzzle that's called Bono, the downright lascivious 'If You Wear That Velvet Dress'. It's emotional stuff, not 'clever' like *Achtung Baby* or, to be more precise, the tour that followed that album.

'Dense' really is a good description of the album. Eno and Lanois introduced space to U2's music. *Pop*'s producers Flood and Howie B seem to have shaped the album out of cement, despite the fact that the band praised Howie B for 'leaving things out' of the mix. Every second of the songs there is something going on, like feedback coming from the deep dark underbelly of Dublin's nightlife. *Pop* has sense of unease, of chaos. It's the sound of something rotten in the state of Ireland.

Ireland and Dublin in particular went through great changes in the Nineties. With European funds pumped into its dormant economy, the country awoke to a vibrant new age. Dublin city, previously frozen in mid-Fifties stupor, was dragged screaming into the Nineties. From raggle-taggle town to mobile toting, pill popping, clubbing centre of Europe. Like any child that's been denied a sweet, the Irish gorged.

No doubt the U2 men enjoyed, indulged and celebrated like everybody else in their city, sampling the pleasures of this new Ireland. They felt the buzz of the burgeoning dance scene. So enchanted were they with their nights out on the town, they opened a club of their own. Located in the former kitchens of their Clarence Hotel, the band created a late night watering hole, The Kitchen. It was a great place to see and be seen, if you managed to negotiate the interesting door policy.

All of these experiences ended up on *Pop*. From the beats and the rhythms, to the drugs and the women, *Pop* reflects the hedonism that followed the first Gulf war and the chaos and confusion of other developments: like the Northern Ireland's peace talks under supervision of Senator George Mitchell, the IRA breaking their 17-month cease-fire with a bomb that killed two in London, the heat of that summer's marching season and the siege at Drumcree. It's certainly one of U2's darker records.

"The themes are love, desire and faith in crisis," The Edge told *Propaganda*, the band's own publication, and Bono added: "Each song is its own little world, that's what this record is going to be like I think. [ ... ] It's very difficult to pin this record down. It's not got any identity because it's got so many." Like liquorice all sorts, it tastes like more.

---

## DISCOTHEQUE

'DISCOTHÈQUE' started as a jam between The Edge and Howie B. Fusing rock and electronics and borrowing from dance U2 end up sounding like a mental metal version of the Miami Sound Machine. This comic sounding opening song and first single off the album is one in a long line of U2's little ditties about addiction. Here, U2 tap into the zeitgeist and the reality of night time Dublin. The superficial pleasures of the dance floor are all referenced ('love doves' are ecstasy tablets), but there's more to it. Be it drugs, God, love, sex or getting out of our heads on live music, we all want heaven in our hearts. These fleeting moments of euphoric forgetfulness are there for the taking, but the minute we reach them, they're gone.

## DO YOU FEEL LOVED

MORE STATEMENT than question, 'Do You Feel Loved' looks at sex as communication – conjuring up a sweaty 'tangle of a conversation' with lovers 'sticking together'. It's a celebration this turning the act 'into your own prayer'; a prayer to a lover or an audience or God who has got the singer's 'head filled with songs'.

The song is based on the band Naked Funk's 'Alien Groove Sensation', a record released on Howie B's Pussyfoot label. Howie spun the record in the studio as a rhythm track (Larry being away due to his back problem) and the band jammed on top of it. Naked Funk are credited on the sleeve for 'inspiration' and if you compare the two tracks they're unmistakably similar, but somewhere underneath the dense production the song nervously echoes rhythms and shards of melodies we heard on *War*, specifically 'Surrender' and 'Two Hearts Beat As One'.

---

## MOFO

JAZZ LEGEND Jimmy Scott sang it the best: "Sometimes I feel like a motherless child." Lyrically inspired by a conversation Bono had with his friend Simon Carmody about the word 'motherfucker', Mofo takes an obscene cliché and turns it on its head. Bono's spilling desperate,

Bono on guitar during 'Zoo TV', 1993.

Zooropa, 1993.

Bono in 'Zoo TV'.

Bono and The Edge with Brian Eno and Luciano Pavarotti at the
September 1995 War Child charity concert in Modena, Italy.

The *Passengers* soundtrack (1995), and *Pop* (1997).

The Edge of stage during the 'Pop-Mart' tour, 1997.

Adam during 'Pop-Mart'.

Larry on stage at Ft Lauderdale, Florida, March 26, 2001, during the 'Elevation' tour.

Bono and Adam at the Gelredrome Stadium, Arnhem on the Netherlands, July 2001.

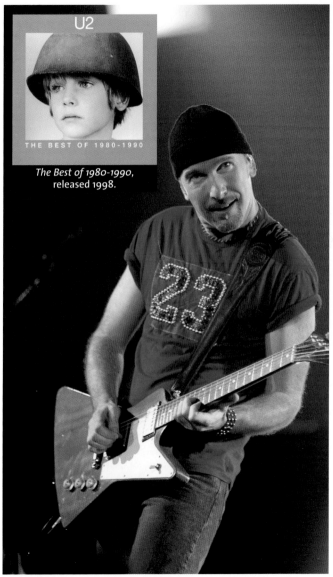

*The Best of 1980-1990,*
released 1998.

The Edge on stage during the 'Elevation' tour, at Anaheim, California,
April 26, 2001.

*All That You Can't Leave Behind*
(2000).

U2 arrive at Schipol Airport, Amsterdam, for their concerts in July 2001.

fragile lyrics packaged in funky industrial noise. "My whole life is in that song," he told Q magazine. Bono lost his mother when he was in his teens. "It's a very desperate lyric," he says, "but it has a bit of swagger to it to sweeten the pill. It's about the reason why I'm in a band – and why a lot of people who I meet have taken up electric guitar or whatever it is. There is a hole that you're attempting to fill as a painter, or a filmmaker or a shouter in a rock group, and that's how you turn the pain of what's happened to you in your life into some kind of blessing."

The Christian philosopher Blaire Pascal believed that every man has a God-shaped vacuum in his heart which cannot be filled by any created thing, but only by God. There is a reference to this idea in the song's first verse: "Looking for to fill that God shaped hole", though some claim Bono picked it up from Salman Rushdie. There's a bit of Yeats in there as well, from his poem A Woman Young And Old: "I'm looking for the face I had Before the world was made." It all comes to a head in the song's spoken middle eight where the tortured inner child of the rock star asks: "Mother... am I still your son, You know I've waited for so long to hear you say so, Mother... you left and made me someone, Now I'm still a child, no one tells me no."

## IF GOD WILL SEND HIS ANGELS

WRITTEN from the point of view of a woman in a relationship gone sour, this bleak 'science fiction country' ballad has its roots in the Zooropa sessions. The female protagonist asks her abusive husband not to blame anyone for their situation but themselves. All around her she finds the world corrupt and in a crisis of faith she wonders: "... where is the hope and where is the faith, and the love" (1 Corinthians 13:13), before issuing a final plea for God to send her a sign, something to hang on to. In the background, you can hear the woosh of angel wings coming down to save the day.

## STARING AT THE SUN

OASIS were at the height of their popularity when U2 record Pop. The two bands become chummy and Bono surprises singer Liam Gallagher by knowing the words to all Oasis' songs. Musically 'Staring At The Sun' seems to come out of The Edge's interest in the Mancunians' song writing. The acoustic guitar, like Noel's in the Oasis hit single 'Wonderwall', is upfront in the mix. To be fair, the band left their most Oasis-like song off the album: 'Holy Joe' was demoted and released as an extra track on the 'Discothèque' single.

In 'Staring At The Sun', Bono typically combines the personal and the political. It feels like stormy weather in a relationship against the backdrop of marching season in Northern Ireland. This is one of three songs on *Pop* to make reference to the Troubles – the others are 'Wake Up Dead Man' and 'Please'.

The lovers here are once again stuck together. But this time it's 'with God's glue': love. It's *Agape*, charitable love, as opposed to the *Eros* of 'Do You Feel Loved'. The song talks of temptation and 'intransigence all around' – but lovers as well as politicians have to learn how to compromise to live together.

## LAST NIGHT ON EARTH

ANOTHER gem left over from the *Zooropa* sessions, an apocalyptic monster of a tune that did particularly well in the live setting of the PopMart shows. In the studio, the band had some problems finishing the song, Bono finding himself unable to come up with its chorus until a few hours before U2 were scheduled to leave for New York to master the album.

There's something very Irish about its premise, the idea of living each day as if it's your last. In his book *Into The Heart*, Niall Stokes implies this song is about a close friend of the band and Howie B's called Saoirse – which is why they ended up having arguments over the lyrics right up till the end. Gavin Friday comments: "You are at a party or a club and you just don't know where this 23-year-old is getting her energy from. [ ... ] It's just a vibe, a wild woman who gives you a charge of energy."

## GONE

AFTER 'Last Night On Earth's respect and concern for a young woman's lust for life, Bono makes his own defiant statement: "I'm not coming down". He's still a child and no one tells him no. 'Gone' started out as Bono's big two fingers up to the begrudgers, but somewhere along the way it became more than that, apparently influenced by the death of this book's original author Bill Graham, journalist and eloquent champion of the band. Bono's very own 'My Way' ended up a little more self-questioning than originally intended: "You hurt yourself, you hurt your lover, then you discover... what you thought was freedom was just greed." In the end, the song becomes an invitation: "We'll be up with the sun, are you still holding on..." The singer himself says the song's bridge resonates with his friend Gavin Friday's 'The Last Song I'll Ever Sing' (*Shag Tobacco*, Island Records, 1995), written in memory of Dublin street performer Thom McGinty, 'The Diceman', who died in 1994.

## MIAMI

WISH YOU were here? Miami reads as a postcard from The Edge, Bono, Adam and Larry, an account of a business trip that became a spring break. "Creative tourism," says The Edge of their stay in the Sunshine State.

"A man makes a picture, a moving picture, through the light projected, he can see himself up close..." Bono sang in 'Lemon'. In 'Miami' the picture is being made and the result is an amusing vignette of an exciting place to be. Still, home is where the hurt is and despite being on the other side of the planet, Bono – like Al Jolson before him - knows: "When you're all alone, here's what you'll keep saying, when you're far from home: Mammy, Mammy."

## THE PLAYBOY MANSION

B ONO name checks Roy Orbison when he talks about 'The Playboy Mansion', but it sounds more like U2 have discovered *smoove*, the Fun Lovin' Criminals way. This laid back gospel tune brims over with acidic cultural observations and religious references.

Bono draws from *Revelations* 21:4 when he sings: "Then there will be no time of sorrow, then there will be no time for pain..." He is still looking for gold among the trash, looking for meaning in a world where 'prosperity is the new religion'. He wonders whether he's got the gifts to get through the gates of the mansion. If you can't beat 'em, join 'em? On Zooropa, he threw away the key. This time, the mansion's owner has changed the locks.

## IF YOU WEAR THAT VELVET DRESS

T HIS IS one of the tracks U2 began working on with Nellee Hooper in London, which explains its trip-

hop leanings. Both Flood and Howie B later had their way with the tune. From the same deeply personal songbook as 'Promenade', 'Love Is Blindness' and 'Your Blue Room', this late night jazz rumble finds Bono at his most predatory, prowling around reminiscing, reliving, wishing.

Atmospherically the sexual slow dance also reminds us of the *Joshua Tree* B-sides like 'Walk To The Water' and 'Luminous Times (Hold on to love)'. Night time brings forgiveness and healing, while in the daylight the melancholy couple 'struggle for things not to say'. Bono doesn't really have the voice to pull off a Barry White, but Adam sustains the underbelly vibe with a fat bass line..

## PLEASE

B ONO: "What I hate about religious fundamentalists is that they shrink the size of God, they recreate God in their own image, tiny, petty, greedy, pathetic. A fanatic is someone who cares more about ideas than people. And that time and their time, is coming to and end. This is one that I had the misfortune to meet and I wrote this song. Because even worse is when you find that kind of revolutionary coming out a well off middle-class family, that's when it really goes up my nose."

By all accounts it appears this song came relatively easy to the band, working off a basic rhythm idea Howie B had laid down. Yet it's like a mini opera, a complex build up of ever increasing intensity, flowering naturally towards its emotional crescendo: a desperate cry for peace. "Please... please... Let's talk," Bono would whisper like a prayer, performing this song in concert.

Evoking the February 1996 London Docklands bombing, the peace talks 'getting nowhere', hypocrites preaching, the sermon on the mount delivered like a car bomb, yet again the song transcends the Troubles – somewhere in there is another story of lovers and liars and the break down of communication.

## WAKE UP DEAD MAN

NELLEE Hooper worked on 'Wake Up Dead Man' with the band during the *Zooropa* sessions. At the time the song, then called 'The Dead Man', was meant as a B-side. It's a simple slow tune with some unsettling background din, excerpts from 'Besrodna Nevesta' by Le Mystère Des Voix Bulgares –

the State Radio and Television choir from Bulgaria. The choir first entered the world of pop music when record label 4AD released their UK debut in 1986. Compared to the likes of Cocteau Twins and This Mortal Coil, the choir found an audience among fans of those bands.

The song antagonised some of the band's Christian following – particularly because of its first verse: "Jesus, Jesus help me, I'm alone in this world, and a fucked up world it is too." It was the first time a U2 song contained profanity – not only that, it dared mention Jesus in the same breath. Some confused questioning with loss of faith. Bono's shaking his fist at his God. He says: "To me, the song goes back to the idea of (King) David being the first blues singer and the first man on record to shout at God in this angry fashion. There are a lot of people who feel that if there is a God, then roll him out because they've got some questions to ask. It's a very angry song."

# All That You Can't Leave Behind

### Island CIDU212; released October 2000

**O**N THE SOBER MONOCHROME ALBUM SLEEVE OF *ALL THAT YOU CAN'T Leave Behind* a monitor behind the band reads: 'J33-3'. Early versions of the cover art as released to the press reveal that the original sign said 'F21-36', designating the check-in desks at Roissy Hall 2F, Charles de Gaulle airport in Paris, where the photo was taken by Anton Corbijn. The band asked the designers – who describe the look they created as 'grown up' – to change the sign. It's a reference to bible verse *Jeremiah* 33:3, which says: "Call unto me and I will answer thee and show thee great and mighty things which thou knowest not." Bono refers to it as "God's own phone call".

On the picture, Larry's seen cheekily peeking over Bono's shoulder. The singer's lost in thought, contemplating his passport. Or perhaps it is a bible. Adam looks amused, The Edge typically nonplussed. In the background, a mother takes a child by the hand. It's a snapshot of the band in between destinations. Dublin, Paris, the world. Still travelling. Still passengers. Waiting to get on board. In their forties, the men look comfortable. Corbijn says: "It's going back to how U2 are as people... they're very rich, they travel a lot, and they carry luggage." The Dutchman admits he 'arranged' the pose for the band. It takes a lot of work to look that casual.

Near the end of the taxing PopMart tour, Bono told Australian press: "One of the things we've learned is that songs actually travel great distances, faster than all the millions of diodes and pixels that we have on the big drive-in movie screen. I can see the songs connecting. And for me, we've got to make a record that reflects where we're at right now. And where we're at right now is making very direct music, probably to contrast with the circumstances of this tour. I think that's where it'll go for us and I imagine that's what will happen on the next record." It did.

"I'm just trying to find a decent melody," Bono sings in 'Stuck In A Moment You Can't Get Out Of', "a song that I can sing in my own company." Who are Bono's company? For all the people the man meets, the makers and shakers, rock stars and politicians, Bono's real tribe is the band and the extended family that surrounds them: the wives, the kids, the associates and the friends that have stuck with them since childhood.

It is as inspiring as it is amazing how after all these years the members of the band are still friends. They don't just tolerate but genuinely enjoy each other's company and they always end up hanging out together. Whether it is in the South of France or for Thursday football games and 'boys night out' in Dublin – they're an old fashioned Irish clan. It's a group difficult to get in to, as even The Edge's wife Morleigh told the press in a rare interview. At its core, you'll find some of the former members of Lypton Village – these days known as the 'Stankard family'. They take care of their own, the street gang that grew into The Mob. It's what kept them grounded and what's kept them together. It's from this sense of community that the album *All That You Can't Leave Behind* emerges. When Bono's talks about the song 'New York' he insists the character's midlife crisis is not his own. Perhaps not, but it could be. And it could be Gavin's, or Reggie's or The Edge's. They and the other family members have all hit the forty mark and have lived, loved and lost.

Write about what you know. It's sound advice for any writer – it provides all the background you need: a plot, characters and dialogue. Part of the success of what could irreverently be called U2's 'comeback' record, can be attributed to them sticking to this simple rule. The band decided not to go to London or elsewhere this time. The record was recorded in Dublin. Producer Danny Lanois thought staying in the band's hometown interfered with making the record, but he was wrong. The domesticity and directness of the album is part of its universal appeal. *Pop* could be vague in how it drew from the kind of life the majority of U2's audience had no knowledge of. *All That You Can't Leave Behind* is less about romantic rock star notions and more about what's 'real'. It hits you where it hurts the most. At home. "Clever is not as high up on our list as soul," Bono told Danny Eccleston, editor of Q4music.com. The madness that was the Nineties was over. It was time to reflect, time to grow up a little. It's to U2's credit that they realised, as Larry Mullen says: "... there's only a certain amount of Joshua Trees you can chop down."

Coming up to the Millennium, Bono became involved in Jubilee 2000's Drop The Debt campaign. From spraying graffiti on public property to part-time politician seemed a giant leap for a rock star. But Bono's got the mind for it. By summer 2000 he said his work with Jubilee was influencing the material for the new album: "There's a certain joy that I've picked from working with the Jubilee people, and there's a righteous anger, if you want to call it that, that makes for great rock and roll." One of the other things driving the singer surely must have been the desire to set right what went wrong with *Pop*. Paul McGuinness spoke honestly: "The key is to achieve a new and younger audience with each record. It's nice that the older audience is still interested in U2, but the more important part of the audience is definitely the new ones."

*All That You Can't Leave Behind* sits comfortably on the line between commerce and art. Part conscious effort to win back their audience, part divine inspiration, it is a fine piece of work. *All That You Can't Leave Behind* doesn't go against the grain, and it doesn't try to be ahead of its time. It doesn't change the sound of music, it doesn't overly flirt with contemporary trends. Yet it's up front and in your face. Simple in outlook, rich in detail and songs that stick in your head. While some of the younger fans the band gained with *Pop* were disappointed, U2's older fans – in their thirties and forties like the band themselves - found comfort and hope in the new material.

*All That You Can't Leave Behind* is easy to relate to, full of solid songs that appeal to a wide audience with its clear notions of family, friendship, love, death and re-birth. These are themes U2 have explored before, but here they come to the forefront, no longer obscured by supposedly 'difficult' music. More Lanois than Eno on first impression, the sounds on this album come from a band that has digested the music it started to consume while making *Rattle And Hum*. This time they are neither imitating nor paying tribute. This time it's soul music, not music about soul.

Sales of the album hit the 10 million mark worldwide in December 2001. Its first single, 'Beautiful Day', earned Grammy nominations for song of the year, record of the year and best rock performance by a duo or group. Some 24 years into their career, when other bands retire or worse, lose the fire, U2 make the album that even non-U2 fans couldn't help but buy – with a shelf life comparable to *The Joshua Tree*. McGuinness declared happily: "My guess is that this record is going to be bigger than *The Joshua Tree* in the fullness of time."

---

## BEAUTIFUL DAY

IT STARTS with a heartbeat and a ringing riff banged out on The Edge's old Gibson Explorer – much used up until *The Unforgettable Fire* but a little out of favour since, backed by a Spectoresque choir singing harmonies. The first single off the album is a breath of fresh air on the radio and unashamedly U2.

"Tá an lá go h-álainn," the Irish say in greeting, "It's a beautiful day": a positive way to start a conversation and just the thing to tell a friend down on his luck. Bono says it's about a person who loses everything and has never been happier. It's about taking stock of the important things in life and finding beauty after the floods. To do so, you sometimes need a different perspective. Bono takes it to extremes, adopting an astronaut's view during the bridge: "See the world in green and blue". It's an idea that's been with him for a while. "When you see the Earth as this little blue marble, the perspective you have on yourself and on the planet is so dra-matic," Bono said to Niall Stokes, talking about 'Your Blue Room' from *Passengers*.

---

## STUCK IN A MOMENT YOU CAN'T GET OUT OF

'STUCK' came out of a piece of music Edge had made and a lyric Bono was writing that had lived separately for a long time until one late night they both found out their separate efforts just might work together. "When you are in the studio," says the guitarist, "it's really a case of looking for opportunities and piecing together clues until you sort of figure out what the songs are trying to tell you. And this is a case of just arriving at that tune from two different directions."

Brian Eno predicted 'Stuck In A Moment You Can't Get Out Of' would be U2's biggest selling single. He was wrong, but that doesn't make it any less great a song. Featuring one of Bono's best vocals, this smooth rock ballad borrows from the Philly sound, though it goes easy on the brass. It wouldn't have felt out of place on *Rattle And Hum*. Bono refers about 'Stuck' as "an argument between mates", trying to shake them out of their misery. Drawn from the death of INXS's Michael Hutchence, 'Stuck' is 'All That You Can't Leave Behind' in a nutshell. It takes the most personal of experiences – the death of a friend and the guilt you feel – and turns it into something widely accessible and comforting to all.

## ELEVATION

A LIVE BAND needs a song to kick off a concert and 'Elevation' sounds like it was written purposely with that in mind: offer the audience a tune that gets them going, then feed off the energy they return. What to think of throwaway lyrics like "a mole, digging in a hole, Digging up my soul now, going down, excavation"? 'Elevation' just about out-pops *Pop*. You know what? It's better not to think about it that much. Just put your hands in the air and wave 'em like you just don't care.

## WALK ON

T HE BURMESE leader Aung San Suu Kyi and her struggle for free elections in Burma inspired Bono to write 'Walk On'. Aung San Suu Kyi left her home in Oxford, her job her son and her husband to return to Burma and fight for her people at great danger to her own safety. It was, according to Bono, one of the great acts of courage of the 20th

century. At first he tried to write the song from the point of view of her family, but in the end he decided to keep it a little more abstract so it could be a love song about someone "having to leave a relationship for the right reasons".

## KITE

" I HAVE HEARD the big music and I'll never be the same, something so pure just called my name..." Mike Scott wrote for The Waterboys' 1984 album *A Pagan Place*. The phrase Big Music launched a genre, and possibly a very bad haircut. U2 were part of it, so were The Alarm, Simple Minds and Big Country in the days that synth-pop rules supreme. When they bought the axe that felled the Joshua Tree, big music went down with it and the band survived the Eighties with their musical integrity intact. But everybody loves an old fashioned U2 anthem and on *All That You Can't Leave Behind*, U2 subtly bring back a little of that hope and glory sound. 'Kite' is the best example. Built on a string arrangement The Edge worked up on the sequencer, it's classic U2, with the added value of the singer's matured voice and insights.

The Edge gets a lyric writing credit on this song, he helped Bono out when he got stuck. "It seems I knew what he was writing about and he didn't," he says. 'Kite', triggered by a trip to the beach with the kids, is a song about family and parenthood; about Irish men and their

Irish fathers. Though Bono's father had influenced his writing before (a number of tracks on *Zooropa* come to mind) it was never as pronounced as on 'Kite' and never as upfront as when Bono wrote about his mother. Bob Hewson had been ill for some time and his sons were now forced to take care of him the way he tried to when they were kids and their mother died. 'Kite' looks at all of this, switching perspective from father to son, from son to daughter. And the boy who wouldn't be told 'no' screams "I'm a man, I'm not a child." When your parents go, you're nobody's child.

While helping Bono with the lyrics The Edge also managed to come up with one of his most emotionally affecting guitar licks ever. It no less than electronic keening and goes straight to the tear ducts, if Bono's howl hadn't already taken you to that place.

At the end, Bono takes a step back from the big emotion of the song by putting a time stamp on it: "... when hip hop drove the big cars, in the time when new media, was the big idea," capturing this personal moment for himself, for the future.

## IN A LITTLE WHILE

RECORDED on a Friday morning after a great piss up on the ritual boys' night out, this slow burn love song of old acquaintance and years gone by has Al Green written all over it, and what a wonderful thing it is. Sometimes the drink can loosen up the voice and though he sounds raw, Bono hits all the big high notes. The song's given a little pop lift by the post production of producers and songwriters Richard Stannard & Julian Gallagher, known for their work on chart toppers Atomic Kitten, Kylie Minogue and David Gray.

## WILD HONEY

AFRAID the album would become too heavy on the listeners' heads, the band decided to include a more upbeat tune. 'Wild Honey' is just that – crafted in the way of fan favourites 'Spanish Eyes' and 'Angel Of Harlem'. Unlike those two hits, 'Wild Honey' can't boast of the accolade. It has Bono swinging from trees like a monkey, stealing honey from the bees and sending flowers all in hope of a roll in the hay with his loved one. All that delivered in a way that suggest neither the singer nor the band can quite believe they're recording this. Just the sort of a happy tune that reminds you that sad songs are the best songs.

## PEACE ON EARTH

'WAKE UP Dead Man' part II? Bono does little to hide the bitterness as he spits out the words "peace on earth". Musically reminiscent of 'One Tree Hill', this is no Christmas carol, like 'Sunday Bloody Sunday' wasn't a rebel song, like Springsteen's 'Born In The USA' wasn't as patriotic an anthem. Swiping and twisting a line from Seamus

Heaney's translation of Sophocles' *The Cure At Troy* ("And hope and history rhyme"), Bono laments the victims of the August 15, 1998 Omagh bombing and reflects the despair felt throughout the nation on that day and wonders if there's a God in heaven, what is he waiting for?

## WHEN I LOOK AT THE WORLD

SOME of us are sinners, some are saints. Some turn the other cheek, some throw bricks through a window. Bono, the aggressive pacifist, is in awe of those who have peace within, those who have grace. Acknowledging his own impatience, he can't do without them. Someone like his wife Ali perhaps, who is committed to The Chernobyl Children's Project. He sings: "... without you it's no use, I can't see what you see."

It was thought having children would mellow Bono, but he says:"'Far from it. I got more intense in a lot of ways about the way I saw the world, my determination to get to grips with it. It's the lengths you would go to protect your children. My pacifism, my hallmark in the Eighties, was challenged by having children. I try to channel that into activism."

## NEW YORK

QUITE A few characters inhabit the world of 'All That You Can't Leave Behind', and they're not the luckiest bunch. There's the man

who has lost everything in 'Beautiful Day', there's the person leaving a relationship in 'Walk On', there's the friend who's at the end of his tether in *Stuck In A Moment*. And here we have the bloke having his midlife crisis in New York. Bono has on several occasions insisted it's not himself he is talking about – this man losing his balance and his wife. Is it the 'Beautiful Day' character again?

Full of images of sinking ships, this person's crisis is of Titanic proportions. Searching for escape he succumbs to the lure of the city, a modern day Loreley whispering "come away". (There's Yeats again, *The Stolen Child*: "Come away, O human child! To the waters and the wild.") The Edge's seductive backing vocals echo the feeling.

Both an ode to the city (there's a hint of Sinatra's 'New York, New York' in there and originally the idea was to have it segue into a bit of that tune) and a song of regret, musically New York is a nervous U2 epic – from the same songbook as 'Exit', if a little less dark.

## GRACE

GRACE IS "... the name for a girl, it's also a thought that changed the world", a tribute to the woman in 'When I Look At The World'. A hymn to her as well as to the idea. Bono first mentioned the idea of grace publicly during the Jubilee campaign. He spoke of debt relief as "... a historic act of grace, an idea to give a billion people a fresh start."

The concept of grace, God's unconditional love and favour, is the reason Bono "would like to be a Christian" he told *Rolling Stone*'s Anthony DeCurtis. Grace reaches all men, rejects none and "lives outside of karma" because God's love is so overwhelming, no matter how evil your sin you will be forgiven. Grace "carries a pearl", God's gift to humanity: the kingdom of heaven.

'Grace' was one of the last songs U2 finished during the sessions, built on an early groove that was shelved for the longest time. In the end, Lanois wrote the guitar part and Eno the keyboard. Together, the band created a soothing song to close the album on a peaceful note.

# COMPILATIONS
# U2 The Best Of
# 1980-1990

**Island CIDDU 211; released November 1998**

**DISC ONE:** 'Pride (In The Name Of Love)', 'New Year's Day' (edit), 'With Or Without You', 'I Still Haven't Found What I'm Looking For', 'Sunday Bloody Sunday', 'Bad', 'Where The Streets Have No Name', 'I Will Follow', 'The Unforgettable Fire', 'Sweetest Thing' (single mix), 'Desire', 'When Love Comes To Town', 'Angel Of Harlem', 'All I want Is You', 'October', 'One Tree Hill'

**DISC TWO:** 'The Three Sunrises', 'Spanish Eyes', 'Sweetest Thing', 'Love Comes Tumbling' (version II), Bass Trap (instrumental), 'Dancing Barefoot', 'Everlasting Love', 'Unchained Melody', 'Walk To The Water', 'Luminous Times (Hold On To Love), Hallelujah Here She Comes', 'Silver And Gold', 'Endless Deep', 'A Room At The Heartbreak Hotel', 'Trash, Trampoline And The Party Girl'

U2'S FIRST *BEST OF* ALBUM WAS PART OF A DEAL WITH ISLAND RECORDS FOR three *Best Of* compilations, announced in September 1998. The band signed the contract while Seagram's/Universal Music were in the middle of taking over Polygram, who owned Island Records. U2 switched to Interscope Records for the US market, but their *Best Of* contract meant this and future hits albums are to be released on the Island label.

The track list of U2's first compilation album runs like a fan's wet dream of a live concert set list. It's 'Golden oldies' U2 style: 14 tracks picked from *Boy* to *Rattle And Hum*, with the song 'October' tagged on as a 'hidden' track for good measure. 'Sweetest Thing', a B-side from the *Joshua Tree* era, was revamped to become the single promoting the compilation.

The CD focuses on the late Eighties with only one track off *Boy* and one (hidden) track off *October*. This means that older fans' favourites such as 'Gloria', 'Tomorrow', 'Out Of Control', '11 O' Clock Tick Tock', 'An Cat Dubh' and 'The Electric Co' were left off. Anyone of these could have taken the pace of 'When Love Comes To Town' on the compilation. *Rattle And Hum* is over-represented with no less than four songs. That's a little over the top, even if the album is better than the film.

Even if you already owned all or most of the album tracks on the 'Best of', it's worth getting for the B-sides compilation disk, though you may want to skip track six, a rather pedestrian cover of Patti Smith's 'Dancing Barefoot'. We're also not too sure of the band's versions of 'Everlasting Love' and 'Unchained Melody'. Perhaps these classic songs should be left alone. Fans keen on the atmospherics on *The Unforgettable Fire* will love 1987's 'Walk To The Water' and 'Luminous Times'. The former shows that U2 were jazz men before they ever worked on the *Million Dollar Hotel* soundtrack, or penned 'Conversations On A Barstool' for Marianne Faithful.

*U2: The Best of 1980-1990* was released in November 1998 in two formats. A 'limited edition' double CD with a second disc of 15 B-sides which was only to be available during the first week of release after which a single 'Best Of' CD without the extra B-sides disc would become available. Exactly how limited the 2-CD version actually was is unclear... 'not very' would be a fair estimation. The double set was later re-released some areas.

At the time the two-disc set became the highest selling greatest hits collection by any band in its first week of release and I reached Double Platinum status with two million copies sold.. It entered the charts at number one in 17 countries, including Canada, UK, France, Australia and Japan. In Ireland it stayed in the charts for 76 weeks.

All the tracks were digitally remastered from the master tapes where possible. Some songs were edited especially for the compilation. 'New Year's Day' is an edit from the Japanese 7-inch single. 'The Unforgettable Fire' is slightly edited down from the original version on the album while 'When Love Comes To Town' comes in at 4:17 instead of the original 4:15.

Four5One's stylish gold, black and white artwork of both the single and the compilation features Ian Finlay's photographs of Peter Rowan, Bono's friend Guggi's younger brother who had already been immortalised on *Boy*, *War* and various early singles. The rich look complements the CD's contents – a fine representation of the band's early work.

## THE SWEETEST THING

ORIGINALLY recorded in September 1988, this bittersweet love song in a tasty pop wrapper was written by Bono to say 'sorry' to his wife Ali whose birthday he had missed while in the studio. That sentiment is reflected in the video for the 1998 version. During the Elevation tour Bono told his audience from the stage that Ali had asked if she could have the rights to the single's proceeds. She agreed to appear in the video (which also features Irish boyband Boyzone and Bono's brother Norman). The money went towards The Chernobyl Children's Project, to which the singer's wife has devoted much of her time.

The Edge told Q magazine the band had originally left the song off The Joshua Tree because it was so different. "Afterwards we realised it should have been on the album." Steve Lillywhite finished the track originally produced by Lanois and Eno., adding new vocals and additional instrumentation.

# U2 The Best Of 1990-2000

**Island CIDZU213 – 063361-1; released November 2002**

**DISC ONE:** 'Even Better Than The Real Thing', 'Mysterious Ways' (Best Of 1990-2000 version), 'Beautiful Day', 'Electrical Storm' (William Orbit mix), 'One', 'Miss Sarajevo' (single edit), 'Stay' (Faraway, So Close!), 'Stuck In A Moment You Can't Get Out Of', 'Gone' (Mike Hedges mix), 'Until The End Of The World', 'The Hands That Built America', 'Discotheque' (Mike Hedges mix), 'Hold Me, Thrill Me, Kiss Me, Kill Me', 'Staring At The Sun' (Mike Hedges mix), 'Numb' (Mike Hedges mix), 'The First Time', 'The Fly'

**DISC TWO:** 'Lady With The Spinning Head' (Extended Dance mix), 'Dirty Day' (Junk Day mix), 'Summer Rain', 'Electrical Storm', 'North And South Of The River', 'Your Blue Room', 'Happiness Is A Warm Gun' (Gun mix), 'Salome' (Zooromancer mix), 'Even Better Than The Real Thing' (Perfecto mix), 'Numb' (Gimme Some More Dignity mix), 'Mysterious Ways' (Solar Plexus Club mix), 'If God Will Send His Angels' (Big Yam mix/Grand Jury mix), 'Lemon' (Jeep mix), 'Discotheque' (Hexidecimal mix)

U2 FINISH WORK ON THE *BEST OF 1990-2000* ALBUM IN LATE JULY 2002. It's the second under their deal with Island records for three such compilations. The Edge revealed to fans outside their recording studio on Hannover Quay that the band were working on a single for Christmas and that they were – and he seemed most excited about this little fact – remixing the *Pop* album. Three of these remixed *Pop* tracks end up on the A-side compilation: 'Discothèque', 'Staring At The Sun' and 'Gone'. It also includes a new version of 'Numb'.

Both 'Discothèque' and 'Gone' are brought closer to their live incarnations while 'Gone' also features different lyrics from the original version. "What you thought was freedom is just greed" becomes "What you thought was freedom just was greed." It's debatable whether the 2002 Mike Hedges remixes improve on the original versions. 'Gone' does seem punchier, but all the life is sucked out of 'Discothèque'. The Edge: "The album version borrowed a lot from dance music and the aesthetics of dance music and what was going on at that time. But this version is back to the band, the essence of what U2 is about. It's more reminiscent of the way that song was performed live. I think it's more to the point." I respectfully disagree. The song has its fun disco balls cut off – it may be the essence of the band, but it still leaves the tune emasculated. One wonders whether this rewriting of history makes sense at all.

I was delighted to see all of the band's work of that decade represented more or less equally. They didn't skip over their more 'European' sounding release *Zooropa* as feared. 'Stay' is simply one of the band's best songs, up there on a lonely height with perhaps only 'One' to keep it company. And the inclusion of the underrated track 'The First Time' tells me someone in U2 still has their head together. It's a song of family and friendship that, musically as well as thematically, fits in well with the more recent material off *All That You Can't Leave Behind*. 'Miss Sarajevo' makes an appearance too – hey, wasn't that a *Passengers* tune? U2 own up and reclaim their orphaned song.

Too bad they left 'The Ground Beneath Her Feet' off in favour of the awful 'The Hands That Built America'. 'Hands' really wasn't meant to be a stand alone song, if you ask me. It may work in the context of Scorcese's film, but outside of that it's a little weak. The new song on the compilation, however, more than makes up for it: 'Electrical Storm' shines like a star in Bono's summer night.

For the first week of sales, stores offered a three disc set containing an A-sides and a B-sides disc and a DVD which promoted the *Best of 1990 – 2000 DVD*. In the second week a single (A-sides) disc version became available. In the UK and Japan the A-sides CD contained 'The Fly' as an extra track, probably to encourage fans to buy the local release rather than the often cheaper imports. Some fans complained about the fact that 'The Fly' was demoted like that, but apparently the band thought that song hadn't aged well.

The B-sides disk unfortunately doesn't include 'Slow Dancing' or 'Two Shots Of Happy, One Shot Of Sad' and instead offers a number of dreary 'extended' and 'perfecto' mixes of standards like 'Mysterious Ways'. We aren't too keen on the version of 'Lady With The Spinning Head' either. Thankfully the Salomé mix leaves the song intact. First heard on the *Achtung Baby* outtakes, it's still sexy as hell and by far the most danceable of U2 songs. Which can't be said of the mismatch that is Big Yam Mix of 'If God Will Send His Angels', which sounds like the worst kind of home grown mash up. Is it me, or were U2's B-sides more interesting the previous decade? Thankfully, *Passenger's* 'Your Blue Room' makes it to the compilation as well, for the fans who didn't want to fork out for Original Soundtracks 1. Immediately after 'Your Blue Room' the band slaughter The Beatles' 'Happiness Is A Warm Gun', but not in a bad way. It's rap influenced cover, twice as long as the original.

Perhaps not as immediately appealing a compilation as U2's first *Best Of*, it does contain some of their best material, all taken from a decade that is considered their most 'experimental'. 'One', 'Stay' and 'Mysterious Ways' are as much 'classic U2' as 'New Years Day', 'I Will Follow' and 'Where The Streets Have No Name'. These are the songs that will stand the test of time. The new song included on the A-sides disk, 'Electrical Storm' serves as the bridge to the next decade of U2's career – set to launch Spring 2004 with a new album.

Speaking to *Billboard* magazine to promote the compilation, The Edge said: "... it's very much, I think, a song of the moment; it's also, I think, a connecting point to our next record. I really think that, in terms of arrangement, it's really back to guitar, bass, and drums, the primary colours of rock'n'roll, I think that's where we're going to take the next album." Late 2003 reports on the material U2 have recorded for their new album suggest The Edge's hunch was right.

---

## ELECTRICAL STORM

A POST 9/11 love song, 'Electrical Storm' is one of U2's best singles with a strong melody, impassioned vocals and words that stick in your brain. "You're in my mind, all of the time..." Bono croons and you feel he means it. "Baby don't cry," he pleads. But the music makes you want to weep. In a good way.

The song was played on the radio long before intended. Bono had sent a demo of the song to a DJ friend on her wedding day. Sarah Cox played it on BBC Radio 1, two months before release. The mix she got featured an acoustic guitar driven track. U2 in the meantime was working on a mix with William

Orbit who gave the song a dreamy glockenspiel start. A third 'band' mix – in which the acoustic is replaced by an electric guitar ended up on the B-sides disk. Unfortunately, the rather appealing Radio1 mix was never released.

"It's about a couple in a room," Bono says, "feeling a storm brewing in the sky outside and equating that to the pressure they feel in their relationship. I think it captures a sense of unease I feel around the world, especially in America, an air of nervous anticipation. It's not an overtly political song, but I don't think we could have written it before what happened in New York.'

---

# SINGLES/EPS & EXTRA TRACKS

**F**OR THE SIXTIES GENERATION, B-SIDES WERE A TEST OF A BAND'S CALIBRE. In an era when top quality non-album singles were a regular currency, The Beatles and the Stones regularly offered excellence on their flipsides as well. Today's paying punter, however, is usually dealt a hand of superfluous re-mixes and warmed over live tracks. As for U2, their surplus tracks are often fascinating if usually unkempt and unfinished. Usually, they've been U2 in the raw, raucously adventuring down new avenues that sometimes turn out to be cul-de-sacs but which can also later prove to be the first if unsteady steps into a new area of operations.

It doesn't really happen with their earliest material. 'U23' is, of course, their legendary, limited edition and exceedingly rare début 12-inch for CBS Ireland that includes early versions of *Boy* tracks, 'Out Of Control' and 'Stories For Boys'. Otherwise the most interesting tracks lurking on the reverse side of their early singles are 'J.Swallow' on the back of 'Fire', the closest the early U2 got to the music of their Lypton Village companions, The Virgin Prunes; and the bizarrely titled 'Treasure (Whatever Happened To Pete The Chop)' on the back of 'New Year's Day', a nifty pop number with Edge's usual guitar tricks unaccountably absent. 'Celebration', backed by 'Trampoline, Trash And Party Girl', is the only other early single that didn't transfer to album.

With the arrival of Brian Eno in the producer's chair, U2 started to stretch out. Even so, it's easy to see why both 'Boomerang', on the flip of 'Pride...', and 'Bass Trap' on 'The Unforgettable Fire' 12-inch, didn't qualify for the album since both are rather more Eno than U2. The first is rather too obviously Talking Heads while on the second ambient piece Edge gets to play Robert Fripp for a restful day. But 'Love Comes Tumbling', presented with both singles, stakes out new ground as a fetching, almost Parisian, pop song in its basic, bare design. That U2 didn't know how to follow its tail; today's would. 'Three Sunrises' is the other orphan from those sessions. With its massed vocal harmonies and jolting guitar, it obviously didn't fit the album's mood.

On the *Joshua Tree* sessions, a new passion emerged on the bonus tracks. They're more compressed, grittier than the official album tracks and almost seem to be Bono's own private exorcism. 'With Or Without You' was suitably accompanied by two other love songs to his wife. 'Luminous Times (Hold On To Love)' is intense and apparently improvised. 'I love you because I need to, not because I need you,' Bono shouts with brave emotional honesty. As for 'Walk To The Water', this rap is a lost gem, filled with memories of early Dublin.

For 'I Still Haven't Found...', the accompanying 'Spanish Eyes' verges on Texas bar-room rock and with 'Where The Streets Have No Name', U2 offered 'Race Against Time', an urgent, almost industrial groove of an instrumental, flecked by backwards Esperanto vocals from Bono. Also in that single's 12-inch package was their own first version of 'Silver And Gold' just short of the compressed conviction of the later live version on *Rattle And Hum*; and 'Sweet Thing', another soulfully improvised concoction.

Two conclusions can be drawn from the *Rattle And Hum* surplus. Firstly, both the extra originals could have made it to the album. 'Hallelujah (Here She Comes)' is gospel-rock driven by springy acoustic guitars not unlike The Hot House Flowers. 'A Room At The Heartbreak Hotel', with its obvious Elvis Presley reference, is both chaotic and claustrophobic. By its finale Edge is as dirty as he got on *Achtung Baby* while the back-up trio of Edna Wright, Maxine and Julia Waters are wailing to the max. How would *you* like to wake up in a fleapit Memphis hotel with a Jimi Hendrix impersonator and a trio of gospel shouting chambermaids outside the door? Also, the band now embarked on a series of bizarrely eclectic covers, usually cooked up with Paul Barrett in Dublin's STS Studios. Patti Smith's 'Dancing Barefoot' is both fun and prophetic: (a) because Edge gets to show off an impressive Neil Young imitation and (b) because it's U2 playing grunge in 1989.

Another set of covers came with 'All I Want Is You'. Their version of Love Affair's 'Everlasting Love' can only be mischievous playing with their earliest pop memories, while 'Unchained Melody' is Bono uncertain whether he's singing behind Phil Spector or a karaoke machine. Another duo of covers, the Stones' 'Paint It Black' and Creedence Clearwater Revival's 'Fortunate Son' backing a superior recording of 'Who's Gonna Ride Your Wild Horses', were far less outrageous.

But by now U2 were also using their B-sides to experiment in the dance area. The 'U2 3-D Dance Mix', released for promotional purposes only, gave three *Rattle And Hum* tracks to Louis Silas Jnr. to remix. He slotted in exerts from a Little Richard sermon and sax from David Koz on a version of 'When Love Comes To Town' to show how traditional R&B values and rhythms need not be alien presences on the contemporary dancefloor. 'God Part II' and 'Desire' were similarly customised.

Then when 'The Fly' was released, Edge and Bono seized the opportunity to release a passage, 'Alex Descends Into Hell For A Bottle Of Milk', from the soundtrack for the RSC's theatrical adaptation of Anthony Burgess' *A Clockwork Orange*. The package with 'One' included a fetching and almost inevitable cover of 'Satellite Of Love', a remix of their version of Cole Porter's 'Night And Day' for the *Red Hot + Blue* project plus one original, 'Lady With The Spinning Head' which, intentionally or not, took them into Primal Scream territory.

Two other fine tracks from the *Achtung Baby* era were rescued when 'Even Better Than The Real Thing' was released. 'Where Did It All Go Wrong' had frilly neo-psychedelic harmonies while 'Salome' was straight but toothsome R&B, doubtless out of sync with the album's Euro themes.

Two other releases deserve mention. Another set of tracks with 'Who's Gonna Ride Your Wild Horses' resurrected 'Salome' with a flowery dance-mix and also included a fascinating Bono miniature, an impressionistic cover of Presley's 'Can't Help Falling In Love' with just Paul Barrett's keyboards and a skeleton rhythm machine track accompanying blurred and bewitching vocals. Then a double CD format for 'Stay...' included another Bono-Edge sketch, just vocals and acoustic guitars on the Texas waltz of 'Slow Dancing'. The release also came with fierce and impressive live versions of 'Bullet The Blue Sky' and 'Love Is Blindness'.

This account is necessarily selective but it must also mention U2's lone live EP, *Wide Awake In America* with its searing version of 'Bad' and soundcheck recording of 'A Sort Of Homecoming'. I've also excluded the four members' guest recordings outside U2 but three other cameos must be mentioned: a cover of 'Maggie's Farm' on Live For Ireland, the 1986 Dublin Self Aid concert; 'Christmas (Baby Please Come Home)' on the Jimmy Iovine 1987 charity project *A Very Special Christmas*; and, 'Jesus Christ', their Woody Guthrie cover on *A Vision Shared*, a 1988 compilation devoted to the songs of Guthrie and Leadbelly.

---

*C*AROLINE VAN OOSTEN DE BOER WRITES: IN 1994 BONO COLLABORATED WITH Gavin Friday and Sinead O'Connor on the soundtrack of Jim Sheridan's film *In The Name Of The Father*. This is modern Irish music at its best, hi-tech dance meets a celtic tribal dawn – protestant lambegs and catholic bodhrans battling it out.

The following year U2 contributed 'Hold Me, Thrill Me, Kiss Me, Kill Me' to the *Batman Forever soundtrack* It has Bono, as his alter ego MacPhisto, singing an essay on celebrity. It's also an ode to glamrock, Bono did always fancy Bolan.

'Staring At The Sun' packs good value with the songs 'North And South Of The River' and 'Your Blue Room' (for those who wouldn't want to fork out for the *Passengers* album). 'North And South Of The River' was co-written by Christy Moore, who recorded it twice: once on his solo album *Graffiti Tongue* and once – this time with added vocals by Bono and Edge, for a single release.

A cover of M's 'Pop Muzik', which was used at the start of all the PopMart concerts appears on the 'Last Night On Earth' single, as well as mad trip hop grunge version of The Beatles' 'Happiness Is A Warm Gun' – twice as long as the original and with a pushy Bono singing slightly but naggingly off key.

The *Please/Popheart* EP, released a month before the 'Please' single is quite sought after as the live tracks on it, 'Please', 'Where The Streets', 'With Or Without You' and 'Staring At The Sun', capture the band at their best.

'If God Will Send His Angels' didn't really work as a single, but is worth mentioning for a re-recording of 'Slow Dancing', the song Bono penned for Willie Nelson and the one he wrote for Frank Sinatra, the beautiful 'Two Shots Of Happy, One Shot Of Sad'. The fourth track on this single is a rare opportunity to hear The Edge sing an acoustic version of 'Sunday Bloody Sunday', recorded in Sarajevo.

The first proof that U2 hadn't lost their muse after their PopMart struggle came in 2000 with the release of the soundtrack to the Wim Wenders film *The Million Dollar Hotel* (scripted by Bono). Bono executive produces the soundtrack and members of U2 appear on most of the tracks, most notably on 'The Ground Beneath Her Feet' (lyrics by Salman Rushdie), 'Never Let Me Go' and 'Stateless', a song that thematically foreshadowed the travelling theme of the *All That You Can't Leave Behind* album and tour.

The first single off the 2000 album 'All That You Can't Leave Behind' contained two new songs. The bitter sweet 'Summer Rain' would have fared well on the album instead of 'Wild Honey', but 'Always' was disappointingly based on the same backing track as 'Beautiful Day'. Lyrically it was a little more interesting, with references to the temptation of Christ ("put your head over the parapet") and its conviction of the need to take risks.

"As long as you're on your knees and she's not on her back" - Bono's oral fixation - gets another outing in 'Big Girls Are Best' on the 'Stuck In A Moment' single, a fun track that seems to be a left over from the *Pop* sessions, produced by Howie B and Flood. It has that mid-Nineties Oasis dirty feel about it.

There are too many 'Elevation' single releases to mention, but one of them has U2's 'rub-a-dubbalin' cover of Johnny Cash's 'Don't Take Your Guns To Town.'

As if the glam rock pastiche of 'Hold Me, Thrill Me, Kiss Me, Kill Me' wasn't good enough, Gavin Friday and Maurice Seezer enlist Bono to sing on their version of T-Rex's 'Children Of The Revolution' for Baz Luhrman's film *Moulin Rouge*.

The US only Target release 7 is an EP containing seven songs which had been released on various formats in Europe, but were unreleased in the US. It's mostly interesting for the acoustic version of 'Stuck In A Moment'.

'The Hands That Built America' is the song U2 wrote for Martin Scorcese's film *The Gangs Of New York*. With its references to 'freckled hills' and hesitant melody it works in the context of the film, but did it deserve its Oscar nomination? It appeared on the *Best of 1990 - 2000* album and DVD before the soundtrack release. A single release was planned but eventually withdrawn. Finally, I must make mention of the Bono penned lyrics for the ballad 'Time Enough For Tears', music by Gavin Friday and Maurice Seezer, for Jim Sheridan's intensely personal drama In America. It is sung by Andrea Corr, whose watery voice follows logically on the film's pre-teen narration. The words read like a Seventies French chanson and speak of the end of summers and autumn leaves. "It's OK, it's OK," she ends on a whisper. And you know it will be, come springtime.

# U2: EP & SINGLES DISCOGRAPHY
## EP

### WIDE AWAKE IN AMERICA
Bad (live)/A Sort Of Homecoming (live)/Three Sunrises/Love Comes Tumbling
*Island 90279 (12 inch)  May 1987*

Bad (live)/A Sort Of Homecoming (live)/Three Sunrises/Love Comes Tumbling
*Island CIDU 22 (CD)  May 1987*

# SINGLES

**U23**: Out Of Control/Stories For Boys/Boy-Girl
*CBS 7951 (Ireland only 7 inch) September 1979*

**U23**: Out Of Control/Stories For Boys/Boy-Girl
*CBS 127951 (Ireland only 12 inch) September 1979*

Another Day/Twilight
*CBS 8306 (Ireland only 7 inch) February 1980*

11 O'Clock Tick Tock/Touch
*Island ILWIP 6601 (7 inch) May 1980*

A Day Without Me/Things To Make And Do
*Island WIP 6630 (7 inch) August 1980*

I Will Follow/Boy-Girl
*Island WIP 6656 (7 inch) October 1980*

Fire/J. Swallo
*Island WIP 6679 (7 inch) June 1981*

Fire/J. Swallo/Cry/The Electric Co. (live)/11 O'Clock Tick Tock (live)/
The Ocean (live)
*Island UWIP 6679 (double 7 inch) June 1981*

Gloria/I Will Follow (live)
*Island WIP 6733 (7 inch) October 1981*

A Celebration/Trash, Trampoline And The Party Girl
*Island WIP 6770 (7 inch) March 1982*

New Year's Day/Treasure (Whatever Happened To Pete The Chop)
*Island WIP 6848 (7 inch) January 1983*

New Years Day/Treasure/Fire (live)/I Threw A Brick (live)/
A Day Without Me (live)
*Island UWIP 6848 (double 7 inch) January 1983*

New Years Day/Treasure/Fire (live)/I Threw A Brick (live)/
A Day Without Me (live)
*Island 12WIP 6848 (double 12 inch) January 1983*

Two Hearts Beat As One/Endless Deep
*Island IS 109 (7 inch) March 1983*

Two Hearts Beat As One/Endless Deep/Two Hearts Beat As One
(US Mix)/New Years Day (US Mix)
*Island ISD 109 (double 7 inch) March 1983*

Two Hearts Beat As One/Two Hearts Beat As One (US Mix)/New Years Day
(US Mix)
*Island 12IS 109 (12 inch) March 1983*

Pride (In the Name Of Love)/Boomerang II
*Island IS 202 (7 inch) September 1984*

Pride (In The Name Of Love)/Boomerang II/4th Of July/Boomerang I
*Island ISD 202 (double 7 inch) September 1984*

Pride (In The Name Of Love)/Boomerang II/4th Of July/Boomerang II
*Island ISX 202 (12 inch) September 1984*

Pride (In The Name Of Love)/Boomerang II/4th Of July/Boomerang II/
A Celebration (live)
*Island CIS 202 September 1984*

Pride (In the Name Of Love)/Boomerang II
*Island ISP 202 (7 inch picture disc) September 1984*

Pride (In The Name Of Love)/4th Of July/ Sunday Bloody Sunday/Love Comes
Tumbling/60 Seconds In Kingdom Come
*Island U2PACX 3 (double 7 inch) April 1986*

The Unforgettable Fire/A Sort Of Homecoming (live)
*Island IS 220 (7 inch) April 1985*

The Unforgettable Fire/The Three Sunrises/Love Comes Tumbling/
Bass Trap
*Island 12IS 220 (12 inch) April 1985*

The Unforgettable Fire/Love Comes Tumbling/
60 Seconds In Kingdom Come
*Island ISD 220 (double 7 inch) April 1985*

With Or Without You/Luminous Times/Walk To the Water
*Island IS 319 (7 inch) March 1987*

With Or Without You/Luminous Times/Walk To the Water
*Island CIS 319 (cassette) March 1987*

With Or Without You/Luminous Times/Walk To the Water
*Island 12IS 319 (12 inch) March 1987*

With Or Without You/Luminous Times/Walk To the Water
*Island CID 319 (CD) March 1987*

I Still Haven't Found What I'm Looking For/Spanish Eyes/Deep In the Heart
*Island IS 328 (7 inch) April 1987*

I Still Haven't Found What I'm Looking For/Spanish Eyes/Deep In the Heart
*Island ISJ 328 (12 inch) April 1987*

I Still Haven't Found What I'm Looking For/Spanish Eyes/Deep In the Heart
*Island CID 328 (CD) April 1987*

Where The Streets Have No Name/Silver And Gold/Sweetest Thing
*Island IS 340 (7 inch) August 1987*

Where The Streets Have No Name/Silver And Gold/Sweetest Thing
*Island CIS 340 (cassette) August 1987*

Where The Streets Have No Name/Silver And Gold/Sweetest Thing/Race Against Time
*Island 12IS 340 (12 inch)  August 1987*

Where The Streets Have No Name/Silver And Gold/Sweetest Thing/Race Against Time
*Island CID 340 (CD) August 1987*

In God's Country/Bullet The Blue Sky/Running To Stand Still
*Island S7-99385 (US only)  November 1987*

One Tree Hill/Bullet The Blue Sky/Running To Stand Still
*Island K 338 (New Zealand only)  November 1987*

Desire/Hallelujah (Here She Comes)
*Island IS 400 (7 inch)  September 1988*

Desire/Hallelujah (Here She Comes)/Desire (Hollywood mix)
*Island 12IS 400  (12 inch) September 1988*

Desire/Hallelujah (Here She Comes)/Desire (Hollywood mix)
*Island CIDP 400 (CD picture disc)  September 1988*

Angel Of Harlem/A Room At The Heartbreak Hotel
*Island IS 402 (7 inch)  December 1989*

Angel Of Harlem/A Room At The Heartbreak Hotel/Love Rescue Me (live)
*Island 12IS 402  (12 inch)  December 1989*

Angel Of Harlem/A Room At The Heartbreak Hotel/Love Rescue Me (live)
*Island CDPD 402 (CD picture disc)  December 1988*

When Love Comes To Town/God Part II (Hard Metal Dance Mix)
*Island IS 411 (7 inch)  April 1989*

When Love Comes To Town (Kingdom Mix)/
God Part II (Hard Metal Dance Mix)
*Island 12IS 411 (12 inch)  April 1989*

When Love Comes To Town (Kingdom Mix)/
God Part II (Hard Metal Dance Mix)
*Island CIDX 411 (CD)  April 1989*

When Love Comes To Town (Kingdom Mix)/
God Part II (Hard Metal Dance Mix)
*Island CIDP 411 (CD picture disc)  April 1989*

All I Want Is You/Unchained Melody
*Island IS4 22  (7 inch) June 1989*

All I Want Is You/Unchained Melody
*Island ISB 422  (7 inch in box) June 1989*

All I Want Is You/Unchained Melody
*Island CIS 422 (cassette)  June 1989*

All I Want Is You/Unchained Melody/Everlasting Love
*Island 12IS 422 (12 inch) June 1989*

All I Want Is You/Unchained Melody/Everlasting Love
*Island 12ISB 422 (12 inch in box) June 1989*

All I Want Is You/Unchained Melody/Everlasting Love
*Island CID 422 (CD) June 1989*

The Fly/Alex Descends Into Hell For A Bottle Of Milk
*Island IS 500 (7 inch) November 1991*

The Fly/Alex Descends Into Hell For A Bottle Of Milk
*Island CIS 500 (cassette) November 1991*

The Fly/Alex Descends Into Hell For A Bottle Of Milk/The Lounge Fly Mix
*Island 12IS 500 (12 inch) November 1991*

The Fly/Alex Descends Into Hell For A Bottle Of Milk/The Lounge Fly Mix
*Island CID 500 (CD) November 1991*

Mysterious Ways/Mysterious Ways (Solar Plexus Magic Hour Remix)
*Island IS 509 (7 inch) December 1991*

Mysterious Ways/Mysterious Ways (Solar Plexus Magic Hour Remix)
*Island CIS 509 (cassette) December 1991*

Mysterious Ways/2 Remixes
*Island 12IS 509 (12 inch) December 1991*

Mysterious Ways/4 Remixes
*Island CID 509 (CD) December 1991*

One/Lady With The Spinning Head
*Island IS 515 (7 inch) February 1992*

One/Lady With The Spinning Head
*Island CIS 515 (cassette) February 1992*

One/Lady With The Spinning Head/Satellite Of Love
*Island 12IS 515 (12 inch) February 1992*

One/Night And Day/Satellite Of Love
*Island CID 515 (CD) February 1992*

Even Better Than The Real Thing/Where Did It All Go Wrong
*Island IS 525 (7 inch) May 1992*

Even Better Than The Real Thing/Salome
*Island CIS 525 (cassette) May 1992*

Even Better Than The Real Thing/Perfecto Mix
*Island 12IS 525 (12 inch) May 1992*

Even Better Than The Real Thing/Salome/Where Did It All Go Wrong
*Island CID 525 (CD) May 1992*

Who's Gonna Ride Your Wild Horses (Temple Bar Edit)/Paint It Black
*Island IS 550 (7 inch) November 1992*

Who's Gonna Ride Your Wild Horses (Temple Bar Edit)/Paint It Black
*Island CIS 550 (cassette) November 1992*

Who's Gonna Ride Your Wild Horses (Temple Bar Edit)/
Paint It Black/Fortunate Son
*Island 12IS 550 (12 inch) November 1992*

Who's Gonna Ride Your Wild Horses (Temple Bar Edit)/
Paint It Black/Fortunate Son
*Island CID 550 (CD) November 1992*

Lemon (Bad Yard Club Mix/Version (Dub)/Momo's Reprise/
Perfecto Mix/Jeep Mix
*Island 422825 957-1 (US only 12 inch) September 1993*

Stay (Faraway So Close)/I've Got You Under My Skin
*Island IS 578 (7 inch) November 1993*

Stay (Faraway So Close)/I've Got You Under My Skin
*Island CIS 578 (cassette) November 1993*

Stay (Faraway So Close)/I've Got You Under My Skin/
Lemon (Bad Yard Mix)/Lemon (Perfecto Mix)
*Island CID 578 (UK CD) November 1993*

Stay (Faraway So Close)/Slow Dancing/Bullet The Blue Sky (Live)/
Love Is Blindness (Live)
*Island CIDX 578 (UK CD) November 1993*

Stay (Faraway So Close)/I've Got You Under My Skin
*Island 422858 076-4 (US cassette) November 1993*

Stay (Faraway So Close)/I've Got You Under My Skin/
Bullet the Blue Sky (Live)/Lemon (Bad yard Mix)/Love Is Blindness
*Island 422858 C97-2 (US 5 inch CD) November 1993*

Hold Me Thrill Me Kiss Me Kill Me (Single Version)/
Themes from Batman Forever (Non U2)
*Island-Atlantic 7567-87131-7 A7131 (UK 7 inch) June 1995*

Hold Me Thrill Me Kiss Me Kill Me (Single Version) /
Themes from Batman Forever (Non U2)
*Island-Atlantic 7567-87131-4 A7131C (UK Cassette) June 1995*

Hold Me Thrill Me Kiss Me Kill Me (Single Version) /
Themes from Batman Forever (Non U2) / Tell Me Now (Non U2)
*Island-Atlantic A7131 (UK CD) June 1995*

Hold Me Thrill Me Kiss Me Kill Me (Single Version) /
Themes from Batman Forever (Non U2)
*Island-Atlantic 7567-87131-4 (US Cassette) June 1995*

Hold Me Thrill Me Kiss Me Kill Me (Single Version) /
Themes from Batman Forever (Non U2) / Tell Me Now (Non U2)
*Island-Atlantic 2-87131 (US CD) June 1995*

Hold Me Thrill Me Kiss Me Kill Me (Single Version)
*Island-Atlantic 2-87125 (US CD) June 1995*

Miss Sarajevo (Single Version) / One (Live from Modena)
*Island IS625 (UK 7 inch) November 1995*

Miss Sarajevo (Single Version) / One (Live from Modena)
*Island CIS625 (UK Cassette) November 1995*

Miss Sarajevo (Single Version) / One (Live from Modena) /
Bottoms (Watashitachi No Ookina Yume) / Viva Davidoff
*Island CID 625 (UK 5 inch CD) November 1995*

Miss Sarajevo (Single Version) / One (Live from Modena) / Bottoms
(Watashitachi No Ookina Yume) / Viva Davidoff
*Island CID 625 (US 5 inch CD) November 1995*

Discothèque (DM Deep Extended Club Mix) / Discothèque (DM Deep Beats
Mix) / Discothèque (DM TEC Radio Mix) / Discothèque (DM Deep
Instrumental Mix) / Discothèque (12' Version) / Discothèque (David Holmes
Mix) / Discothèque (Howie B Hairy B Mix) / Discothèque (Hexidecimal Mix)
*Island 12IST649 (UK Triple 12 inch) February 1997*

Discothèque (12' Version) / Holy Joe (Garage Mix)
*Island CIS649 (UK Cassette) February 1997*

Discothèque (12' Version) / Holy Joe (Garage Mix) / Holy Joe (Guilty Mix)
*Island CID649 (UK 5 inch CD) February 1997*

Discothèque (DM Deep Club Mix) / Discothèque (Howie B Hairy B Mix) /
Discothèque (Hexidecimal Mix) / Discothèque (DM Tec Radio Mix)
*Island CIDX649 (UK 5 inch CD) February 1997*

Discothèque (12' Version) / Holy Joe (Garage Mix)
*Island 422-854 774-7 (US 7') February 1997*

Discothèque (DM Deep Club Mix) / Discothèque (Hexidecimal Mix) /
Discothèque (DM Deep Instrumental Mix) / Discothèque (Radio Edit)
*Island 422-854 789-1 (US 12 inch) February 1997*

Discothèque (12' Version) / Holy Joe (Garage Mix)
*Island 422-854 774-4 (US Cassette) February 1997*

Discothèque (12' Version) / Holy Joe (Garage Mix)
*Island 422-854 774-2 (US 5 inch CD) February 1997*

Discothèque (DM Deep Extended Club Mix) /
Discothèque (Hexidecimal Mix) / Discothèque (Album Version) /
Holy Joe (Guilty Mix) / Discothèque (Howie B Hairy B Mix)
*Island 422-854 789-2 (US 5 inch CD) February 1997*

Staring at the Sun / North and South of the River
*Island CIS 658 (UK Cassette) April 1997*

Staring at the Sun (Album Version) / North and South of the River /
Your Blue Room
*Island CID658 (UK 5 inch CD) April 1997*

Staring at the Sun (Monster Truck Remix) / Staring at the Sun (Sad Bastards
Mix) / North and South of the River / Staring at the Sun (Lab Rat Mix)
*Island CIDX658 (UK 5 inch CD) April 1997*

Staring at the Sun / North and South of the River
*Island 422-854 972-7 (US 7 inch) April 1997*

Staring at the Sun / North and South of the River
*Island 422-854 972-4 (US Cassette) April 1997*

Staring at the Sun (Album Version) / North and South of the River /
Your Blue Room
*Island 422-854 975-2 (US 5 inch CD) April 1997*

Staring at the Sun (Monster Truck Remix) / Staring at the Sun (Sad Bastards
Mix) / North and South of the River / Staring at the Sun (Lab Rat Mix)
*Island 422-854 973-2 (US 5 inch CD) April 1997*

Last Night on Earth (Single Version) / Pop Muzik (Pop Mart Mix)
*Island CIS664 (UK Cassette) July 1997*

Last Night on Earth (Single Version) / Pop Muzik (Pop Mart Mix) /
Happiness is a Warm Gun (The Gun Mix)
*Island CID 664 (UK 5 inch CD) July 1997*

Last Night on Earth (First Night in Hell Mix) / Numb (The Soul Assassins Mix)
/ Happiness is a Warm Gun (The Danny Saber Mix) /
Pop Muzik (Pop Mart Mix)
*Island CIDX 664 (UK 5 inch CD) July 1997*

Last Night on Earth (Single Version) / Pop Muzik (Pop Mart Mix) / Happiness
is a Warm Gun (The Gun Mix) / Numb (The Soul Assassins Mix)
*Island 314-572 053-2 (US 5 inch CD) July 1997*

Please (Single Version) / Dirty Day (Junk Day)
*Island CIS673 (UK Cassette) October 1997*

Please (Single Version) / Dirty Day (Junk Day) / Dirty Day (Bitter Kiss) / I'm
Not Your Baby (Skysplitter Dub)
*Island CID673 (UK 5 inch CD) October 1997*

Please (Live from Rotterdam) / Where the Streets Have No Name (Live from Rotterdam) / With or Without You (Live from Edmonton) / Staring at the Sun (Live from Rotterdam)
*Island CIDX673 (UK 5 inch CD) September 1997*

Please (Single Version) / Please (Live from Rotterdam) / Where the Streets Have No Name (Live from Rotterdam) / With or Without You (Live from Edmonton) / Staring at the Sun (Live from Rotterdam)
*Island 314-572 195-2 (US 5 inch CD) October 1997*

If God Will Send His Angels (Single Version) / MOFO (Romin Remix)
*Island CIS684 (UK Cassette) December 1997*

If God Will Send His Angels (Single Version) / Slow Dancing / Two Shots of Happy One Shot of Sad / Sunday Bloody Sunday (Live from Sarajevo)
*Island CID684 (UK CD) December 1997*

If God Will Send His Angels (Single Version) / MOFO (Romin Remix)
*Island 314-572 188-4 (US Cassette) December 1997*

If God Will Send His Angels (Single Version) / MOFO (Romin Remix)
*Island 314-572 190-2 (US CD) December 1997*

If God Will Send His Angels (Single Version) / Slow Dancing / Two Shots of Happy One Shot of Sad / Sunday Bloody Sunday (Live from Sarajevo)
*Island 314-572 189-2 (US CD) December 1997*

MOFO (Phunk Phorce Mix) / MOFO (Black Hole Dub) / MOFO (Mother's Mix) / MOFO (House Flavour Mix) / MOFO (Romin Remix)
*Island 12IS684 (UK 12 Inch) December 1997*

MOFO (Phunk Phorce Mix) / MOFO (Mother's Mix) / If God Will Send His Angels (The Grand Jury Mix)
*Island CIDX684 (UK 5 inch CD) December 1997*

Sweetest Thing (Single Mix) / Stories for Boys (Live)
*Island CIS727 (UK Cassette) October 1998*

Sweetest Thing (Single Mix) / Twilight (Live from Red Rocks) / An Cat Dubh - Into the Heart (Live from Red Rocks)
*Island CID727 (UK 5 inch CD) October 1998*

Sweetest Thing (Single Mix) / Stories for Boys (Live from Boston) / Out of Control (Live from Boston)
*Island CIDX727 (UK 5 inch CD) October 1998*

Beautiful Day (Album Version) / Summer Rain
*Island CIS766 (UK Cassette) October 2000*

Beautiful Day (Album Version) / Summer Rain / Always
*Island CID766 (UK 5 inch CD) October 2000*

Beautiful Day (Album Version) / Discotheque (Live from Mexico) / If You Wear that Velvet Dress (Live from Mexico)
*Island CIDX766 (UK 5 inch CD) October 2000*

Beautiful Day (Album Version) / Beautiful Day (Album Version)
Interscope 314-562 972-1 (US 12 inch) October 2000
Beautiful Day (Quincey and Sonance Mix) / Beautiful Day (The Perfecto Mix) / Beautiful Day (David Holmes Remix) / Elevation (The Vandit Club Mix) / Elevation (Influx Remix) / Elevation (Escalation Mix) / Elevation (Quincey and Sonance Remix)
*Island 12ISD780 (UK Double 12 inch) July 2001*

Stuck in a Moment You Can't Get Out Of / Big Girls are Best
*Island CIS770 (UK Cassette) January 2001*

Stuck in a Moment You Can't Get Out Of / Big Girls are Best / Beautiful Day (Quincey and Sonance)
*Island CID770 (UK 5 inch CD) January 2001*

Stuck in a Moment You Can't Get Out Of / Beautiful Day (Live from Farmclub) / New York (Live from Farmclub)
*Island CIDX770 (UK 5 inch CD) January 2001*

Stuck in a Moment You Can't Get Out Of / Big Girls are Best / All I Want is You (Live from Manray) / Even Better Than the Real Thing (Live from Manray)
*Island CIDZ770 (France 5 inch CD) March 2001*

Elevation (Tomb Raider Mix) / Elevation (Escalation Mix) / Elevation (The Vandit Club Mix)
*Island CID780 (UK 5 inch CD) July 2001*

Elevation (Tomb Raider Mix) / Last Night on Earth (Live from Mexico) / Don't Take Your Guns to Town
*Island CIDX780 (UK 5 inch CD) July 2001*

Elevation (Tomb Raider Mix) / I Remember You (Live from Irving Plaza) / New York (Live from Irving Plaza) / I Will Follow (Live from Irving Plaza)
*Island CIDY780 (Europe 5 inch CD) July 2001*

Elevation (Tomb Raider Mix) / Elevation (Tomb Raider Mix Video) / Excerpts from MTV's Making the Video (Video)
*Island CIDV780 (UK 5 inch DVD) July 2001*

Walk On (Video Version) / Where the Streets Have No Name (Live from Boston) / Stay (Live from Toronto)
*Island CID788 (UK 5 inch CD) November 2001*

Walk On (Single Version) / Stuck in a Moment You Can't Get Out Of (Acoustic) / Stuck in a Moment You Can't Get Out Of (Video)
*Island CIDX788 (UK 5 inch CD) November 2001*

Walk On (Single Version) / 4 x 30s clips from Elevation 2001 Live from Boston / Walk On (Video)
*Island CIDV788 (UK 5 inch DVD) November 2001*

---

Summer Rain / Always / Big Girls Are Best / Beautiful Day (Quincey and Sonance Remix) / Elevation (Influx Remix) / Walk On (Single Version) / Stuck in a Moment You Can't Get Out Of (Acoustic) [Titled '7']
Interscope 3145867222 (US 5 inch CD) January 2002
Electrical Storm (William Orbit Mix) / New York (Nice Mix) / New York (Nasty Mix)
*Island CID808 (UK 5 inch CD) October 2002*

---

Electrical Storm (Band Version) / Bad - 40 - Where the Streets Have No Name (Live from Boston)
*Island CIDX808 (UK 5 inch CD) October 2002*

---

Electrical Storm (William Orbit Mix) / Electrical Storm Video (Director's Cut) / Interview with Larry Video / Photo Gallery
*Island CIDV808 (UK 5 inch DVD) October 2002*

---

# Index